Art of Giving
— A Way of Life —

ACHYUTA SAMANTA
NATIONAL BESTSELLING AUTHOR

RUPA

Published by
Rupa Publications India Pvt. Ltd 2025
7/16, Ansari Road, Daryaganj
New Delhi 110002

Sales centres:
Bengaluru Chennai Hyderabad
Jaipur Kathmandu Kolkata
Mumbai Prayagraj

P-ISBN: 978-93-6156-209-9
E-ISBN: 978-93-6156-546-5

First impression 2025

10 9 8 7 6 5 4 3 2 1

The moral right of the author has been asserted.

Printed in India

*This book is dedicated to
each and every one who stood by me, helped me in the
smallest of ways, and at the most crucial times in the journey
called life, which has gifted me pain in the past, the passion
to work for people in the present and an undying
hope for the future.*

*It is for all those human beings who believe in the
power of giving—go ahead and give, and spread happiness
and peace in the world. It is for all the fans, followers and
practitioners of the philosophy of the Art of Giving.*

❋

Contents

Foreword

India is home to many spiritual traditions and beliefs, whose shared values are founded on kindness and compassion. We have for centuries cherished giving—whether that be of material, emotional or spiritual value—because we believe sharing multiplies the joys of life. In giving we discover selfless bonds with others. We do not give out of guilt but with feelings of joy and gratitude. Giving from the heart fosters true friendship, trust and respect.

I have known Dr Achyuta Samanta for several years, and he is a good friend of mine. As a fellow Odia, I have had the privilege of visiting KIIT (Kalinga Institute of Industrial Technology) and KISS (Kalinga Institute of Social Sciences) on several occasions. The sight of the sheer number of children studying there, coming from far-flung remote corners of Odisha and receiving free education, is simply awesome and deeply moving. I saw light, hope, future, dignity and freedom shining forth from their beautiful, smiling faces.

The dreams of these children, and the future of India, would never be complete without Dr Samanta. He is a warrior who believes in 'eliminating poverty through education'. With each challenge and heartbreak, he emerged stronger in his resolve to provide free education to these children from less-privileged societies. I call this 'compassion in action'.

I consider myself a socially engaged Buddhist, and I am a firm believer in humanity. A simple act of kindness does not require philosophy, religion, or beliefs. All it needs is common sense and a feeling of sameness with others. We are all the same in our desire to be physically healthy and mentally happy. If we are open and accepting in our hearts, we can always be kind to others.

The true meaning of the Art of Giving is the joy of giving. One does not have to be wealthy; one can just offer a glass of water or help someone cross the street. Everyone can practise the joy of giving. Everyone can make a difference. I am so delighted to know *Art of Giving: A Way of Life*, by Dr Achyuta Samanta, is being released. It will provide much-needed wisdom and practical guidance for today's world. I am sure readers will feel inspired and encouraged and rediscover the joy of giving. Many people who feel a void may find their purpose in life after reading the book.

Sarva Mangalam!

—Gyetrul Jigme Rinpoche
Spiritual Head and Founder,
Padmasambhava Baudh Vihara, Jeerang
TMN Society, Jeerang, Odisha
Ripa International Center, Switzerland
Ripa Center, Moscow, Russia

Introduction

One need not be very rich to give something back to society. Rather, one must experience poverty to know the luxury of giving. Charity is an important tenet in every religion because compassion is essential for every human being. *Daan* in Hinduism and Buddhism, *tithe* in Christianity and *zakat* in Islam uphold the philosophy of giving. One must understand that, as Ben Carson said, 'Happiness does not result from what we get, but from what we give.'

Giving is not always about giving only material goods, which are just one form of generosity. It is rather an attitude of, in the words of His Holiness the Dalai Lama, 'being kind, attentive and honest in dealing with others, offering praise where it is due, giving comfort and advice where needed, and simply sharing one's time with someone—all these are forms of generosity, and they do not require any particular level of material wealth.'

That is what we mean by the 'Art of Giving'. Let it be a value inculcated in every heart, because, according to Winston Churchill, 'we make a living by what we get, but we make a life by what we give.'

This book is divided into two sections—The Philosophy and The Philosophy in Action. One must approach this book as a fundamental truth of life. We come into this world with nothing and leave with nothing; what we do in between defines who we are. My mother used to tell me, *'Jaake loke na kahili bhala, se jivanta jeevane malo,'* meaning 'if people don't praise one in their lifetime for their work, it is akin to living dead.'

How will people praise someone if they don't go beyond

their selfish interests, think of those on the margins and do something consequential for those marginalized? I have devoted my life to the cause of uplifting humanity. I was born into extreme poverty and could have, after gaining some wealth and stability, opted for a comfortable life. However, it was the blessings of God that made me an instrument to go beyond personal needs, live a life of simplicity and help all such 'Achyutas', who could become 'Achyuta Samantas' in life, spreading happiness.

I understood this as a one-line summary of my life—someone who gave to me made me happy when I had nothing; I give to make others happy and inspire. It's not just about giving material resources—a kind word, a pat on the back, a phone call, a smile—everything counts. Life is uncertain, as the COVID-19 pandemic has shown, and we should strive to develop our emotional intelligence as artificial intelligence surrounds us.

The Art of Giving has three sets of relationships: with oneself, with one's immediate surroundings, and with society and the ecosystem as a whole. We need to cultivate each of these to find moments of calm, enjoy giving, detox from blue-light exposure and screens, and practise self-love while spreading love and happiness. This book is simply a beginning. It is not the ultimate solution; there is much more that can be done with its principles. Consider it a starting point.

My Message to the Seekers of Peace

AS HUMAN BEINGS, WE ARE INHERENTLY SOCIAL CREATURES, constantly seeking happiness, peace, harmony and companionship. Regardless of our financial status, peace and happiness remain essential to life. People devote time and energy to achieving these states through various means— spirituality, kindness, gratitude, action plans, mentorship, religion or therapy. Some go deep into forests and hills, practise intensely and search far and wide, only to discover that happiness resides within.

Reflecting on my own journey, I struggled for basic necessities until the age of 25. Today, my struggles are of a different kind—I strive to ensure food security for millions. I will continue this pursuit until my last breath. Throughout my life, I have cultivated a peaceful mind, promoted harmony and maintained a calm demeanour. You will never see me tense or restless. Even as I carry my own sorrows, I try to inspire others. I never lose my temper, and I honour the emotions of everyone I meet, regardless of their status. This inner stability stems from qualities I have nurtured over decades.

For the past 32 years, I have worked 16–18 hours every day without a single day off. By God's grace, I have never suffered from even a cold or fever, nor have I ever felt tired or lonely. I live a simple bachelor life, managing everything on my own, and I am content.

My high energy and positivity not only sustain me—they also energize others. I do not harbour negative thoughts or speak ill of anyone. In adversity, I seek the positive. For two to three hours each day, I engage in spiritual practice—something I have done since childhood. This practice brings me deep peace, happiness and fulfilment—and I'm certain it will do the same for you.

One of the most powerful practices, requiring no investment, is to love people genuinely. Real happiness stems from loving others. When you love truly, there is no room for negativity. Love brings all the peace, joy and connection one could ever wish for.

The words 'Art of Giving' came to me in that precise order—unprompted and powerful. I wasn't even thinking about giving or art at the time. It felt divine, as if the Almighty was sending me a message. The words lingered in my mind.

I began to reflect on my life from the age of five. Though my memories are faint, I remember a childhood full of struggle. I lost my father young, and in the 1970s, our country was going through severe economic hardship, hence social welfare schemes were scarce. My siblings and I grew up in extreme poverty, doing odd jobs in the village and eating only when food was available.

To help others understand the depth of our hardship, I often describe it in two ways: we sometimes went without even one square meal a day and my mother did not own a second sari to change into after bathing. This was our life for nearly 15 years—from 1970 until I graduated in 1984 and pursued a Master's degree in Chemistry.

When the Art of Giving came to me, I realized that everything I had achieved was because of it. This concept isn't about giving away wealth or material goods. It's about the selfless acts—offering a smile, kind words, motivation or assistance. Giving is timeless.

Unknowingly, I had learned and practised this art since

childhood. People around us helped because they saw our suffering. They gave us food, support and comfort. From them, I learnt the power of kindness. In return, I always tried to give back—even without realizing it.

As a boy, I delivered groceries to elderly villagers, performed daily puja at an old woman's house in exchange for breakfast and accepted food from anyone offering it with a generous heart. One lady, from a marginalized caste, often gave me sweets during pujas, knowing I never had such treats at home. Since childhood, I have embraced love and kindness from all quarters and reciprocated with service.

In Class 4, I developed a painful boil on my thumb. Despite the pain, I never missed school. I couldn't plant saplings during our gardening class, but I insisted on watering them with my right hand. The wound left a mark that remains to this day. My teacher noticed my dedication and told the headmaster. 'This boy will do something big,' he said. That moment defined my character: I never cheat, I never shirk responsibility.

The name I carry—Achyuta—means 'the one who does not deviate from the path'. True to that name, I have never wavered from my mission. I once worked tirelessly to earn just one rupee so I could treat four friends to 25 paise each for tea and snacks. No one asked me to do this—life's hardships taught me to find joy in bringing joy to others.

From my school days to post-graduation, I actively organized events and helped others, even when I had little. I didn't realize then that these were acts of giving. Over time, they shaped my character, sharpened my organizational skills and laid the foundation for institutions like KIIT, KISS and KIMS.

Even in playful moments—when I took on comedic roles in village dramas just to make people laugh—I was practising the Art of Giving. There are countless such stories buried in my memory. Giving became part of who I am.

I still remember how a teacher enrolled me in school and gave me borrowed stationery when I had nothing. Others gave me books, comfort and encouragement. I always tried to return their kindness.

They say children reflect their parents, and I believe that to be true. I lost my father at a young age but the stories my mother told me painted a picture of a man known for his generosity. Though he was a modest worker, he sponsored the education of the needy, helped with marriages and gave freely—even borrowing money to help others.

In the 1960s, our village suffered from water shortages. My father and a few villagers built a small dam. To fund this, he sold groceries in Tata Nagar and saved every paisa from the margins, accumulating a thousand rupees—just to help others access water. Instead of spending on his own family's comfort, he invested in the village's future.

He didn't live to see the fruits of his labour, but his spirit lives on in me. I didn't learn directly from him, but his values were passed on through his blood. Like father, like son.

My mother was equally influential. She lived frugally, not out of miserliness, but wisdom. When I gained recognition, she transformed our village of Kalarabanka into a 'Smart Village'. Her quiet strength and values pushed me to help others, continuing the legacy of generosity she and my father lived.

The Art of Giving is not just an act—it's a legacy. It transforms lives across generations. My parents taught me, without words, that giving holds the power to change the world.

Everything I am today is because of the Art of Giving. It is not new—it's ancient, universal and embedded in all religions and philosophies. Yet, in today's world of growing inequality, its relevance has never been greater.

I began consciously giving at the age of 22. I realized it wasn't just about altruism—it was a way to improve society, a path to inner peace and communal joy. It became my lifestyle, my personal revolution.

In a world focused on self-interest, the need to expand our compassion to include the marginalized is urgent. Even a small act of giving can have a profound impact on someone struggling to survive.

This principle has shaped my life and work. Through KIIT, KISS and KIMS, I've aimed to offer more than education or healthcare—I've sought to give people hope, dignity and opportunity. The love I receive from the children I call my own is overwhelming. Their affection is the greatest reward.

Today, I am proud to see over 20,000 staff embodying this spirit. What began as a solitary vision has become a shared movement. The small hill I stood on has grown into a mighty mountain.

The Art of Giving has become a social revolution. It is not confined to grand gestures—it lives in everyday kindness, in each supportive word, in every smile shared. It enriches both giver and receiver, creating an ever-expanding circle of positivity.

This is the legacy I wish to leave behind: a life led by compassion, a community sustained by kindness and a future shaped by the spirit of giving.

—Dr Achyuta Samanta

SECTION I

The Philosophy

1

What is the Art of Giving?

In a world embroiled in greed and corruption, Mahatma Gandhi's 'simple living, high thinking' has become a virtue of the past. In this materialistic society, we all aspire for more—better and bigger houses, cars, comforts and luxury—that only money can buy. But most of us never think about the person on the street dying of hunger because we have chosen to live by denying others the material prosperity that we would like to have for ourselves. Even if we think about them and feel pity, we don't know how to help. The Art of Giving is indispensable in such situations. By unlocking it in everyone, we can create waves of happiness for ourselves and for the society we live in.

The Art of Giving is all about creating an unconditional and sustainable abundance of love, peace, happiness and contentment for others through gestures of kindness and generosity. One must experience poverty to know the luxury of giving. For me, compassion is a two-way street. For all the sorrow, poverty and distress in this world, there are unlimited ways of helping—for making a positive difference. Every religion upholds the Art of Giving and spreading happiness and peace, which have inspired me during my struggles in life. Religion disseminating material goods is just one form of generosity. One can always extend an attitude of generosity to one's behaviour.

The Art of Giving is a concept that emerges from a heart that expects nothing in return, where the pure joy found in the act of giving defines the essence of the initiative. It advocates living simply and bringing smiles to the faces of those who need it most, irrespective of their class or creed. This fundamental principle is sustained both in public and personal spheres. It can be seen as the manifestation of an inner sense that has grown within many who have embraced this concept. Givers experience immense joy in their ability to relieve suffering, especially when their acts are voluntary. The profound joy arises not just from the act itself but also from witnessing how these acts of giving help the recipients overcome life's challenges, with a humble and grateful acknowledgement of the sacrifices made by others. The initiative cannot be fully measured or captured; it represents a spread of joy among millions, transcending borders. The Art of Giving goes beyond mere transactions; it involves severing ties with worldly greed and rising far above ordinary desires and actions.

Behind every act of giving, there is often an invisible force—a guiding principle or divine inspiration. Many are moved by examples of charity and are inspired to give as they respond to promptings that align with their deepest values. This concept aligns with the belief that finding joy in life often involves being placed where one can bless and be blessed. In various religious teachings, such as in Indian scriptures, charity or *daan* holds a prominent place.

Every religion preaches the same ideology of philanthropy, be it the Quran's *sadaqah* or zakat; Buddhism's charity to the needy; Jainism's charity of offering food, saving the lives of others in danger, distributing medicines and spreading knowledge; Judaism's *tzedakah* meaning 'justice' or 'righteousness' to denote charity; Christianity's expression of charity as an essential component of faith; and Zoroastrianism, which considers poverty and suffering as an affliction of evil. Hence, it is the duty of every individual to fight this evil.

The Art of Giving is a profound practice that embodies the essence of selflessness and its significant impact on society, demonstrating how life's greatest joys derive from giving and sharing with others.

Is Giving an Art?

The question of whether giving is an art is intriguing. Nobody today denies the goodness associated with giving; it is widely recognized as the most virtuous and solemn act for both the giver and the recipient, creating a win-win situation. However, is this noble deed an automated human response, or is it a trained process of mental hardwiring aimed at promoting the cause of goodness for humanity? In my view, giving must be mastered as an art and learnt through the process of collective consciousness. There are many cognitive calculations involved in this unfathomable and abstract idea.

A giver should consider how deserving the recipient is. Goals should be set, and the impact of giving should be visible immediately or in the long term. Giving to an undeserving candidate or cause may create more harm than good. Thorough homework must be done before any act of philanthropy. Providing a generous amount of money to young adults, for example, could potentially lead them astray. However, giving is a living and dynamic art. One cannot simply give once and then bask in the glory of its benefits; regular follow-up on the impact is essential. Giving should also ensure the sustainable development of the recipients, eventually bringing them to the other side of the cycle of deprivation.

In the process of giving, both sides receive happiness, albeit to varying degrees. It is an act of generosity and kindness on one side and an act of receiving help to overcome challenges on the other. We often pack and give leftovers that will not be eaten at home to the needy. There is a prioritization of whose needs are greater when giving. We donate used clothes and consider ourselves part of the 'League of Givers'.

However, should giving be publicized in such a way that the recipient feels embarrassed? Or should giving be kept secret to preserve the dignity of the recipient? There is another side to this story. Publicizing acts of giving can motivate several others to engage in acts of benevolence. This phenomenon is known as the 'bandwagon effect'. Giving should be popularized through powerful stories and anecdotes without resorting to publicizing one's entry into the club of givers. Intent is the most crucial element in the process. For those without resources, it is all related to compassion for the community, which can be expressed through a name, voice, smile and purpose. The purpose of giving is related to contentment. It promotes an overall feel-good factor but should be applied subjectively according to the situation. Giving is a skill to be perfected through continuity and is acquired, carried forward, and sustained through practice and practice alone.

The Art of Giving as a Way of Life

The Art of Giving is a way of life. The bliss of giving cannot be experienced through teaching. It has to be felt and realized at one's deeper emotional levels, and that is why it is regarded as one of the most revered human virtues. Mythologies suggest that even before the Palaeolithic man accidentally discovered fire, there was someone who, in order to provide happiness to the human world, sacrificed his own peace and pleasure. Prometheus, the Titan from Greek mythology, stole fire from the gods to help humans overcome their misery.

Prometheus's successful efforts to pass on the secret of fire to humanity angered Zeus so much that he punished him with eternal torture. This passing of the knowledge and experience of fire is interpreted as passing on the secrets of the knowledge of creation. This kind of self-transcendence has always paved the way for enriching human life and for the creation of a better world to live in. The Art of Giving resides in such altars of sacrifice where the self is forever dedicated to the common benefit of others without any expectations of returns. But nurturing such goodwill for the world at large is not always taken kindly, as is evident from the punishment that was meted out to Prometheus.

Knowledge is power. It is also a tool that empowers and enables those who have it to control and manipulate others. Thus, the exchange of knowledge eventually becomes a political battlefield. Knowledge acts as a medium as well as a political device, and that is why it should be disseminated and made available for the smooth functioning of society. Both giving and knowledge are intertwined. They both sow the seeds of spiritual development within human beings. When the right spirit of the Art of Giving is mastered, both the giver and the receiver experience bliss. Giving is not just about the dissemination of tangible properties but also encompasses sharing intangible kernels of knowledge. The Art of Giving, thus, espouses moving beyond individual preferences and contributing to the greater integrity of humanity. This will lay the foundation stone for the progress of humanity and the liberation of people from their self-destructive egos.

Giving with Empathy

Our myopic approach to life is pushing our society towards darkness at an alarming rate. People are choosing to stay in their own cocoon; they assume that their personal prosperity is turning the world into a better place. But that is not true. Though one's own development and prosperity are nothing to be ashamed of, one has to ensure that, with all the positive changes taking place, one does not get lost in the maze of one's own bliss. In our society, individual prosperity and progress are always determined by material possessions and the amount of wealth one has managed to amass, because the possessor of wealth wields influence in society that allows them to twist and tweak the surroundings as they desire.

But with the rise in power, one gradually gets distanced from one's own surroundings. This obsession with self and self-advancement is (un)intentionally responsible for building a web of failed relationships. As humans, we cannot afford to cling to our exclusive planets; we are social beings, and it is important to understand that, without the support and love of our near and dear ones, we will perish. Yet, in an effort to excel in the field of the ephemeral, we turn a blind eye to such an important aspect of life. While climbing the ladder of success, we expect others to empathize with us, but we forget to reciprocate their concern at the right time. We do not realize that no human existence is complete without human contact, and genuine relationships never demand any material compensation. They only need to be showered with sincere emotions, love and concern. The pleasure of giving is encoded in these social behaviours.

Sharing material gains with the needy is a great virtue, but sharing time with and showing genuine empathy towards people who matter is equally significant. The true essence of giving lies in these moments of happiness and appreciation. Tiny gestures like remembering birthdays, being present at someone's special moment or during their most distressed hour, or giving a call without any purpose fill the heart of the recipient with the utmost gratitude and happiness. Moments like these define a true human being. When actions are performed without the expectation of any reward, they help contribute to the greater well-being of society and also develop a sense of inward emancipation. A selfless act always purifies the mind and infuses within us the zeal to move beyond ourselves and focus on our dharma (a combination of moral and spiritual discipline). Then, and only then, can we claim to have understood the true meaning of our human existence.

If one is not appreciated or hailed during their lifetime, it's like living dead.

2

Experiences that Shaped
the Art of Giving

FROM THE DEPTHS OF A TRANQUIL MIND, AMIDST THE
bustling chaos of daily life, and with no sense of urgency,
epiphanies occur. As I walked out of Bengaluru Airport on
17 May 2013, three words suddenly came to mind: Art of
Giving. They echoed in my ears and reverberated throughout
my body. As I sat in the car, headed towards the city, I
realized that everything I had practised and achieved in my
life revolved around the Art of Giving. I was the embodiment
of it. My life can be summarized in those three words. All
the answers to my questions and challenges lay in the Art of
Giving. From the days when I had nothing and relied on the
kindness of others, to the struggles of becoming a self-made
man and establishing not one, but two dream institutions, to
the times of accomplishment when I could have indulged in
worldly pleasures but chose to live a disciplined and simple
life of sacrifice—my life revolves around the Art of Giving.

I made deliberate efforts to institutionalize it and promote
it actively in a structured format, creating a community
of individuals who consciously practise the Art of Giving.
Although this philosophy is not new and is present in all
religions and faiths, I made a conscious effort to conceptualize
and provide a framework for action. It is meant to be
practised every day, in every moment, and in every aspect
of life, regardless of one's financial status, age or phase of

life. However, 17 May became a designated day to reflect on this practice, much like how we live life every day but celebrate our birthday as something special.

People worldwide are encouraged to come together to spread happiness and peace. Followers of this universally applicable philosophy, irrespective of caste, creed, gender, religion, colour, nationality, age, financial background or professional and political affiliations are united by this concept. It serves as a symbol of unity for a world connected through the language of kindness and compassion.

Inequality, a significant source of societal problems and conflicts, is addressed through the Art of Giving. This timeless philosophy has found its way into countless homes and hearts, embracing diversity and inclusivity. From the young to the elderly, from developing nations to affluent households, everyone is touched by the Art of Giving. It is celebrated in all places of worship, such as temples, mosques, churches and gurdwaras. The Art of Giving is a great equalizer, bringing together individuals from all walks of life, from those struggling to make ends meet to those who live comfortably and those with generational wealth. This concept serves as a symbol of unity, intertwining kindness and compassion into a universal language that binds humanity.

Reflecting on my own journey, as someone born into poverty and having lost my father at the tender age of four, I am a living example of the Art of Giving. The peace and happiness derived from practising this philosophy need no proof as it has been attested by countless ancestors and wise individuals throughout history. The present generation, armed with unparalleled intelligence, demands authenticity, logic, and honesty in their pursuits. The widespread acceptance of the Art of Giving serves as a testament to the trust it has garnered. Giving can take various forms—monetary contributions, kindness, smiles, patient listening, encouraging words or motivational gestures. However, giving must be cultivated as an art. I strive to embody humility, ensuring that the act of giving unites both parties as equals. It should be characterized by dignity rather than charity, involving discernment and thoughtful consideration.

The Origin

One early morning in 1969, around 5 a.m., when I was about four years old, I could not understand why suddenly my family members were wailing loudly. Not knowing what to do, I looked inquiringly at the grief-stricken faces around me. Soon, I realized that my father had died in a tragic train accident, leaving behind seven siblings and a widowed wife. I was too young to grasp the concept of death. My father, a petty worker, had left no savings for our family of eight to survive on.

Growing up in a remote village in Odisha, India, my siblings and I faced severe poverty. From the age of five, I started doing odd menial jobs to help my widowed mother and provide comfort to my family where I could, wiping my mother's tears and offering my lap as a bed for my little sister. By seven, I was already sharing the little money I earned with my classmates, keeping just one rupee from my daily wages to buy tea and snacks for my four friends at a nearby tea shop.

As I grew into a young man, during my master's programme at Utkal University, Bhubaneswar, I encountered a moment that would define my character. I gave away ₹300—money given to me by my eldest brother for a college picnic—to a friend who couldn't afford to join. I missed the picnic myself, but the joy of helping my friend was more rewarding. After earning my degree in chemistry, I secured a teaching job at a local college. Besides teaching, I tutored privately, using the income to support my friends and family, often at the expense of my own comfort.

In 1992–93, with just ₹5,000, I ventured to set up two institutions in a rented building. Today, Kalinga Institute of Industrial Technology (KIIT) is a leading university hosting around 40,000 students from around the world, and the other, Kalinga Institute of Social Sciences (KISS), is an institution that transforms the lives of around 40,000 poor, indigenous children by providing free education from kindergarten to post-graduation, including professional education, with full residential and boarding facilities. KISS has been instrumental in bringing smiles directly and indirectly to over a million people, and aims to reach 10 million by 2030.

I have also given back to my village, turning it into a model village equipped with all the amenities of a city. My efforts extend to enriching art, culture, films, literature, spiritualism and many other fields. I continue to provide financial assistance to about 200 school friends every month and have employed another 100 friends in my institutions.

Despite creating so much for society and achieving so much, I live a simple life in a two-room rented house without any personal property and have chosen to remain a bachelor. My only hobby is bringing smiles to the faces of thousands of poor children, irrespective of their caste, creed, or religion. I credit all my accomplishments in life to the philosophy of the Art of Giving, which I silently learnt in childhood and have now made my life's ethos. I passionately believe in the potential of the Art of Giving to bring peace to people's minds in society.

If one is not living for others, one is not living at all—this ideal has guided many apostles, from Lord Buddha to Shirdi Sai Baba and many other saints throughout history. 'That is a philosophy which is prehistoric, embedded deep in the human psyche. It is an indispensable tenet that builds the basis of symbiosis, love, bonding and fraternity,' I often say when discussing the foundational principles of my life's work.

As the founder of KIIT, KISS and the Art of Giving, I have not only philosophized about the Art of Giving but have also turned it into a living, breathing phenomenon, not just a mere campaign. It always resides within us, but it must be actively brought to the surface. The Art of Giving wells from within, as it did for me, having benefitted around 80,000 students at KISS over the years with free quality education and healthcare. My role as a philanthropist hardly requires any introduction, thanks to the large canopy of support we have provided.

I inherited this ideal of living for others from my mother, Nilimarani Samanta, who was not only a pathfinder for our family but also a beacon of hope and courage for the entire village. It was from her that I learnt the profound impact of selflessness and service to others, which later inspired me to formalize this philosophy as the 'Art of Giving'. My mother was more than just a trailblazer for our family; she was an embodiment of egalitarianism, an anti-classist, rejecting oligarchy in all its forms. As I navigated countless challenges in life, she galvanized my spirit and guided me towards becoming a better human being.

Unlike many other arts, which may have certain limitations, the Art of Giving has none. From feeling like a loner to becoming a rallying point for this cause, I have worked to spread this moral construct globally, encouraging countless others to join this 'League of Givers' and embrace this vital truth of life.

My Childhood Poverty

In the small space of our dilapidated two-room house, we— my mother, siblings and I—were staring at an uncertain future. The flickering ray of light emanating from the half-lit broken lantern was perhaps a metaphor for our struggle to survive. We knew that the light would not be there for long as the lamp did not have enough kerosene to last the night. Kerosene was a rare commodity for us and we did not have the luxury to choose between darkness and light.

That night was perhaps the darkest, as it not only restricted our movements even inside the room but also filled us with dread. We could hear trees falling to the strong wind and it only added to our sense of fear. All we could do was submit to our fate. I can't recollect any night worse than that one when it seemed that the fountains of the Great Deep had burst and the floodgates of heaven had split apart. But we neither had Noah's Ark nor the basket that saved Moses. We clung to each other, praying that uprooted trees did not come crashing down on us. As water kept gushing through a hole in the thatched roof, we tried to keep ourselves dry but ended up getting drenched anyway. The cold wind blowing through whatever was left of our home made us shiver uncontrollably in the cold. It seemed like a night for the living dead.

The pangs of hunger robbed us of our sleep, and with little to do our mother kept comforting us in every manner possible. I did not understand then that she was bleeding inside, trying courageously to control her tears. She tried to impress upon us to wait for a while till she could get something to eat. All that she could find was some leftover wet rice and cooked wild spinach. But on that cold rain-soaked night, serving us wet rice was out of the question. She then asked us to wait till she made some pancakes with the flour she had bought a few days ago. I was in no mood to eat that either, for I knew she would make it without any oil, and I would have to eat it without sugar.

I was then too young to realize the pain I had unknowingly

caused her that day. One thing we knew was that our mother was not in a position to provide us with even basic luxuries. All my grumbling stopped when she found the oven and the fuel were filled with rainwater. Never to be cowed down, my mother searched for some puffed rice she had kept for me. She searched but could not find it as by then the lantern had run out of oil. My fear, desperation and helplessness turned into anger against my mother, who never allowed us to buy a matchbox as it was also beyond our reach. Our next-door neighbour always lit our lamps, but that night it was not possible. Being virtual prisoners in our own house, I had no option but to sleep. Hunger, fear and the chill in the air denied us even that.

With all odds stacked against us, she mumbled, 'Remember Jagadish is the Saviour and He rescues the fallen.' In a trembling voice, I wanted to know who Jagadish was. She replied, 'He is the Lord of the Universe—Lord Jagannath. You must chant His name, and you will feel no hunger, nor will any tree fall on our house.'

It was the best she could offer us. Before she could finish, there was a loud noise caused by a falling tree. I cried out, fearing that it would crush us alive. In fear, I started to crawl towards my mother in the dark. I crouched over her, holding her tight to ward off the fear. Without a grain of food in my stomach and eerie things happening around us, I started to chant Lord Jagannath's name. The greater my pangs of hunger, the louder my chants grew.

The night slowly gave way to a new dawn, and the inclement weather began to ease. We mustered the courage to step out and witness the trail of devastation the gale and heavy rain had caused. It was still raining, but the wind was not as strong. To our surprise, we found that lightning had struck a palm tree only a few inches away from our house. 'It could have taken our lives,' my mother said, but

I reminded her that it could not have happened, as I was chanting Jagannath's name.

I showed her the mayhem in the surrounding area and told her we were better placed, with only water pouring down from the roof. We were drenched, but still alive. Our house was damaged, but not destroyed. That might have helped reaffirm my faith in Lord Jagannath. As my eyes turned to the other side of our house, I saw an uprooted banana tree. I hurried to get the bananas. I also wanted to cut the tree and get its soft inner trunk for Mother to prepare some curry. It was a struggle between my hunger and the prospect of getting rid of it. Before I could decide what to do, my mother opened the front door. It was equally devastating. I could see hardly any roof on what were once houses.

What also drew my attention were coconuts lying on the road. Some were still falling from the trees. Mother asked me to collect a few coconuts, but they were not ours. In a struggle between what was right and the pangs of hunger, the latter won that day. With great reluctance, we thought of collecting the coconuts. Had it not been such a moment of despair, Mother would not have allowed us to touch them. Her motherly instinct to feed her children got the better of her ideals that day. She tried to convince me that no one knew which coconut came from which tree. The conflict between rectitude and reality was still within me, but I succumbed to the fact that without the coconuts, we would go hungry for some more days.

As I collected the coconuts, I kept chanting the Lord's name to avoid being injured by a falling coconut. My mother was my strength, and she reminded me that nothing would happen if God wanted to protect us. It was not coconuts alone; we collected bananas, papayas, and even the leaves of the coconut trees that were used to cover the leaking roof. The leaves were also used as fuel.

The exercise left me tired, and I felt hungry again. Even in my hunger, I thought of the blessings of Jagannath. Since then, my devotion to Lord Jagannath has grown manifold, and I started feeling His presence whenever I faced a difficult situation. Maybe it was my faith, or maybe it was His wish to take me where He wanted me to be.

Though I collected the raw materials, it was not possible for Mother to cook, as the oven was still underwater. So, we drank coconut water and ate its tender pulp. Before starting to eat, I called my neighbours to take their share. It was also a way to get rid of my feeling of guilt.

The darkness of the night had eventually given way to sunshine, but today, when I look back, I remember the famous lines from Fyodor Dostoevsky's *Crime and Punishment*: 'The deeper the grief, the closer is God!' Indeed, chanting the name of Lord Jagannath helped me sail through all odds.

I have no hesitation in admitting that ever since my mother introduced me to Lord Jagannath, I felt a new energy in me. I believe that I always enjoy the blessings of Lord Jagannath. Whatever I have been doing for my fellow human beings and society, I believe Lord Jagannath has shown me the way and led me on that path. I strongly believe that He will continue to bless me to do more for society, as I have completely surrendered myself at His lotus feet.

Hunger

Sometimes, when I am alone, the picture of my childhood floats in front of me, and my hands automatically go up to wipe my moist eyes. My struggle with poverty, my resolve to live at any cost, and my mother's blessings are my source of strength. Sometimes people ask me how poverty could be a source of strength since the world knows the poor are powerless and poverty is a weakness. But I turned my weakness into my strength. Poverty can never be quantified. Definitions and divisions like 'absolute' or 'relative' poverty do not reveal the whole truth.

Perhaps I was born into poverty. My father, so benevolent and kind, had become a pauper by helping people beyond his means. In that condition of penury, he died, leaving my mother and seven siblings in the lurch.

My mother raised my siblings and me with courage and determination—working as a maid, threshing paddy to make rice for a few coins, or even collecting wild spinach to cook for us. She did everything to keep us alive. She never forgot that she was a mother with an abundance of love for her children. She was a woman whose natural instincts were soft. Like every mother, she wanted her children to live comfortably, but those were her dreams, and she did not know whether they would one day become reality.

I vividly remember the day I realized the depth of my mother's love. Perhaps she loved me most, but the way it was revealed shocked even her.

After my father's death, my elder brother, who had been living in Jamshedpur, trying to get a job on compassionate grounds, returned home. My mother, seeing her eldest son after a long time, naturally wanted to go the extra mile to make him comfortable. Ours was a home where the food containers were always empty. We were living from moment to moment, without any certainty about what the next day would bring. Since there was nothing in the house, my mother ran to a neighbour to ask for some *chuda* (flattened rice). It was all she could ask for, and all that was likely to be available in my village.

Chuda can quell hunger, but it is bland without any accompaniment, like curd or something sweet. My mother got the chuda from one house, but she did not want to feed her son only chuda. She wanted to add something more.

So, she left the bowl of chuda in the kitchen and rushed to our immediate neighbour to borrow some sugar or jaggery.

At that moment, when I returned from outside to ask my mother for something to eat, I found the bowl of chuda. I was hungry, having slept on an empty stomach the previous night since there had been nothing to eat at home. The bowl of chuda was tempting, and I started eating it.

My mother, entering with a little sugar in her hand, saw me devouring the food she had sourced for her eldest son. In a fit of rage, she picked up a stick and charged at me.

At that moment, she must have felt helpless that she could not give her eldest son anything to eat after his long journey. While running away, I turned to see where she was. Just then, the stick came crashing down above my eye. Blood gushed out of the open wound. My mother fainted at the sight of the blood.

Someone took me to the hospital, and I returned with a small bandage over my eye to see my mother crying, blaming herself for what had happened. It was then that I realized how poverty could break human bonds. I came to understand how helpless my mother was and how much she loved her children. It was not that she loved her eldest son more or was angry with me for eating the chuda, but it was her maternal affection for the son she was seeing after a long time. It was her helplessness at not being able to give her younger son anything to eat the night before.

She hugged me, kissed me and kept blaming herself for being so insensitive. I understood the whole situation, but I could do nothing except wipe the tears from her eyes, trying to say that it was nothing, that the stick had not hurt my eye but only the skin above it.

At that moment, as I tried to console my mother, we both realized we were staring at the ugliest side of poverty and hunger.

Self-made Man

Come festivities and I am surrounded by an unspoken, internal bliss—a nostalgic charm that drives me down memory lanes filled with colours, sounds and emotions. The festive season starts right after Ganesh Puja and continues till the end of the month of *Kartik* in the Hindu calendar. The stories of how I grew up in a village, my school life and my childhood days flood my memory.

About four decades ago, I lived in the remote village of Kalarabanka in the Cuttack district of Odisha. The village was quaint and lacked basic amenities, even electricity. A narrow road by the river ran through the village, with most of the modest houses lined along it. Even with no facilities for a comfortable life, the atmosphere of my village was unparalleled, with its lush greenery, the ever-welcoming Paika River—a tributary of the mighty Mahanadi—warm people and a plethora of temples.

The period of puja was special to every member of the village. Interestingly, the festival in our village dated back over 300 summers. Durga Puja and Kali Puja were the most celebrated among the many festivals we participated in. Families came together; people who worked in far-off places returned home, and it was a time of rituals and bonding. Traditional cakes, sweets and clothes were prepared and distributed. Everyone dressed in newly purchased clothes—a tradition. There was a spring in every step and cheer in every heart.

Our cowshed-like house was situated near the centrally located Durga temple, which created an aura of godliness and devotion amongst us and the entire village. Festivals brought with them fun, frolic, sounds of cymbals, group dances and bustle.

Durga Puja, in particular, brings back memories of my

native village. I spent many pujas with my little sister Iti in our dilapidated house, as my two older sisters had been married off and my mother would visit my elder brother in Jamshedpur.

During that period, new clothes and sumptuous food were luxuries we could not even dream of. We watched as people prepared delicious food and ate it without ever offering us any. We saw people revelling in their own happiness, and we were content seeing them enjoy their own paradise.

Even the poor managed to wear new clothes to the best of their capacity during puja. Iti and I would receive a pair of new clothes from our elder brother, which we wore with utmost pride and happiness, continuing to use them until the next festive season. Staying alone, I would cook a plain meal of dalma (lentil and vegetable soup) and rice, stretching it out over the five days of the festival. Somehow or the other, we made ends meet, finding happiness in the little things.

Durga Puja in our village was memorable for another reason: the fair. People from nearby areas gathered to celebrate the joyous and traditional mela. I would set up a small stall and sell balloons with Iti's help; this gave me a source of income without the load of doing a double shift of school and work. It started when I was in class four and continued till the end of my school life. At the end of each day, I would count the money I had earned. Fortunately, I earned a little surplus every time. This income used to give me immense joy as it was hard-earned and honest, no matter how much it was. Though we were poor, my mother always taught us not to cheat or be dishonest or aim for easy money.

Kali Puja was celebrated in my village with greater fervour and zeal. It was an even bigger affair, with a large fair held during the puja. Food, fun and frolic filled the air. Numerous food stalls were set up, offering a rare chance for villagers to enjoy freshly prepared street food. People working outside returned home, making it a time for reunion with family and friends.

Iti and I would go to the fair, roam around and have fun with our relatives and friends. We witnessed the splendour, but we never demanded what we could not afford. Our own relatives pampered their children with aloo chop, bora and rosogullas but never offered us even a morsel. From this time, I understood the humiliation a child faces when they have no support system to fall back on.

No relative ever gave us a chocolate, sweet or balloon—even during festivals. We watched parents shower their children with love, pampering them with goodies and treats, while we looked on from afar. We felt the lack of such a cushion, but we never complained. We never sought sympathy.

I remember those days clearly—and that's why, today, I do everything I can to bring smiles to the faces of millions of children. My only passion is to spread happiness among the deprived. I never forget to give *bakshish* to 1,000 people and provide financial assistance to the needy. During Kali Puja, I distribute sweets, snacks and goodies to the children at two schools in Kalarabanka, which we set up. I also never miss a chance to distribute food to the children in my village. Today, I am blessed to have risen from a balloon seller to a medium of change, alleviating poverty and suffering through education.

God has given me the privilege to return to the same village and spread smiles among the children. Bringing joy to them gives me immense pleasure. It offers me a sense of comfort to know that these children won't feel the sting of deprivation as I once did.

But one thing remains unchanged—then and now—I continue to find happiness in spreading joy and hope.

I carry these memories with me every day. A man is the sum of his experiences, and I am no exception. Though

I am sometimes saddened by the glaring inequalities in society, I accept that the five fingers on a hand are never the same. I have learnt that small acts of giving can spread happiness. The power of good intentions can heal melancholy and uplift society. From my own struggles, I have come to understand the pain of deprivation. In my small way, I have tried to ease the suffering of those at the margins of society—so they can stand on their own feet and lead dignified lives.

One should never forget the past. I always remember what my mother used to say: 'Thili kana, heli kana, hebi kana'—always keep in mind what you were, what you are and what you will be.

Being Human and Humane

Humaneness is a small word, yet its connotation can never truly capture the depth of its importance. It is the core value behind the progress of civilization and the human race—intrinsic and innate to all. In simpler, traditional societies, human bonds were stronger and life was less complicated. However, as we have transitioned into modern and ultra-modern lifestyles, the respect for humanity seems to be diminishing. Ironically, the higher one rises, the less one tends to think about human connections. This is the paradox of our times.

Humaneness, as a value, must be given renewed impetus. Small acts of benevolence can create enormous ripples of change. They can wipe away tears, spread joy and bring smiles. They bring immense pleasure to both the giver and the receiver. The satisfaction one derives from small and random acts of kindness and compassion is nothing but the essence of humanitarianism. Misery and agony can be alleviated by being humane. Having grown up with the core values of humaneness and service, they have become the guiding ethos of my life. I constantly strive to extend support to the needy and distressed.

I aim to offer not only immediate relief but also permanent solutions to those in need. While the sufferings of society seem endless, we can each do our bit. At times, I find myself lost in nostalgia, recalling the kindness shown to my family during its darkest days. Today, it feels as though life has come full circle.

I still remember with extreme pain the day my father died in a train accident, leaving behind seven children and a widowed wife. We had no land, no home and no money. I was only four years old, while my youngest sibling was barely a month old. The devastating news reached my elder brother at 5 a.m. He was 16 at the time. He rushed to the hospital, clinging to hope, but was faced with the stark reality of our father's lifeless body, covered with a white sheet. Seeing him brought my brother back to reality—a moment of shattering grief.

He returned home to seek my mother's consent to claim the body and bring it back for the last rites. My mother, only 40 years old, nodded in stoic silence. She had no idea how she would cope with such a tragedy. Suddenly, the burden of raising seven children amid poverty, hunger and humiliation fell upon her shoulders. She had no support system. Her life was devastated by this cruel stroke of fate. Though some relatives came to offer condolences, no words could console a heart so broken.

In the midst of our grief, a few *kabuliwallahs* (traditional moneylenders) came to our house to recover the small loans my father had taken—borrowings my mother was unaware of. They were known for being ruthless when debtors defaulted. Yet, when they saw our destitute state—the loss of our sole breadwinner and the stark poverty of our family—they left without uttering a word, abandoning all hope of recovering their money. Even those known for their harshness showed compassion.

A few colleagues of my father came home to condole my father's death. I still carry the memory of their kindness. Aware of our plight, four of them came forward, not merely with words of comfort, but with tangible support. They brought us basic groceries and vegetables, ensuring that we did not starve. Their gesture of humaneness kept us afloat.

The prospect of being homeless loomed over us. But then, a distant relative, despite living in a cramped one-room house, offered us his veranda and kitchen as shelter. For six months, we lived there. That small act of kindness anchored us in a time of despair and gave us a sliver of hope. Without it, our family of eight would have been lost—unseen and unrecognized. The compassion extended to us allowed us to survive, to dream and to ultimately thrive.

Great individuals are often shaped by the touch of humaneness they have experienced in their lives. It costs nothing, yet its returns are manifold, enriching the soul and elevating society.

Let me conclude with the words of Desmond Tutu: 'Do your little bit of good where you are; it's those little bits of good put together that overwhelm the world.' Let us embrace this wisdom, for it holds the power to make both our lives and the world a kinder, more compassionate place.

Laying the Foundation of KIIT

In the foothills of the Himalayas, listening to the chirping of birds, my mind was growing restless amid the calm and stunning setting. The serene atmosphere offered no solace to my racing thoughts. Sleepless and restless, I found myself thinking about the previous night's journey.

I was at the Mayfair Himalayan Spa Resort, a spectacular celebration of luxury and heritage located in the hill town of Kalimpong, West Bengal. I had taken time out from my busy schedule to attend the parliamentary standing committee meeting on coal and steel there. Everything was perfect, but then a strange whirlpool of thoughts disturbed my otherwise calm composure. I feel compelled to share the experience of that night.

On my way to Kalimpong, I took a train to Kolkata on the night of 28 August. From there, I boarded a flight to Bagdogra, followed by a three-hour car drive from the airport to Kalimpong. The train journey was very comfortable, but I couldn't sleep as images from the past flashed through my mind.

From 1992 to 1995, during the formative years of KIIT Industrial Training Institute (KIIT-ITI), I had to travel to Kolkata four times a month to procure lab materials and equipment. I did not have money to buy a ticket for sleeper class, let alone an air-conditioned coach. My journeys to Kolkata were mostly in general class on the Jagannath Express, and I rarely had the luxury of getting a seat. On several such trips, I would stand the whole night, sometimes near the smelly toilets and compartment doors, occasionally closing my eyes out of a desperate need to sleep. If luck was on my side, I would manage to find just enough space to squeeze in my slender body or receive an offer to sit after standing for three to four hours.

As I remembered the past train journeys I had taken over the previous 26 years, one particular trip stood out. I was travelling with P.K. Sahoo, a founding member of the staff at KIIT-ITI, to Kolkata by train in general class. It was August 1992. We reached Kolkata in the morning. We had neither a place to stay nor the money to book one.

'My friend's house is a stone's throw away. We can

complete our morning rituals there,' Sahoo Babu had told me in a composed tone.

Beggars can't be choosers. In those days, my condition was more pathetic than a beggar's because I did not have the luxury of mercy. I accepted Sahoo Babu's plan at once.

We started walking towards Sahoo Babu's friend's house. The roads were muddy, and we splashed through puddles, trying to avoid potholes. Kolkata is notorious for getting waterlogged during the monsoon. As we walked, it continued to rain, and the overflowing drain water sapped our energy. When we finally reached, we realized it was a quintessential Kolkata slum.

Heaps of garbage lined the streets and we found food rotting in one of the piles close to his friend's house. Hailing from one of the poorest households in a remote village in Odisha, I was no stranger to such surroundings.

'After walking for an hour and a half, we need to take a bath, Sahoo Babu. I don't see any washroom,' I said to him. There was no proper toilet or place to take a bath at his friend's place.

'I am sorry. This is my first visit too. I didn't know it was like this,' Sahoo Babu mumbled. 'Sir, let's bathe in the Hooghly,' he added.

So, we walked to the banks of the river. It took us another hour and a half. The stench was overpowering. The entire area reeked of fresh defecation. Whenever I travelled, my usual practice had been to use the waiting room toilets at railway stations. This is not to say that they were any better.

Without thinking twice, I took off my clothes, wrapped my *gamucha* (a thin coarse cotton towel), forcefully shut my eyes, ears and nose, took a dip and changed into fresh clothes. I had lived in such conditions before, so I could digest the pain of the surroundings and go ahead with the work as planned.

We then went to purchase the equipment for KIIT-ITI at Bowbazar. By the time we finished our work, it was already evening. As we could afford only one porter, both of us carried the equipment on our heads and shoulders until we found a bus.

While returning, I asked Sahoo Babu, 'Why didn't you book a room in a hotel? It would have cost us ₹500.'

'Sir, we are struggling to get money to buy equipment for our institute. Even ₹500 is too much for us. We are taking loans and using them for KIIT-ITI. How can we think of spending it for our comfort just to get a clean toilet?'

I had no answer. I was in a state of denial.

Fast forward to 2018. Twenty-six years later, I was on the same train, divinely blessed with comforts I had never dreamed of. This time, I was in an AC first-class compartment. I could have taken a flight to Kolkata, but my engagements in Bhubaneswar compelled me to take the last possible train. The station master came to see me off. My staff and colleagues came to bid me farewell, and the train attendants extended unmatched hospitality.

I went to the toilet, cleaned up, and did not have to do my bedding because the attendant had made all the arrangements. However, I could not sleep because I was reminded of the night on the same train to Kolkata and my state of helplessness then. My heart swelled with gratitude to the Almighty, who made me work hard and achieve whatever I have—for millions and myself.

I thanked all the gods for giving me a life of comfort.

I was trying to sum up life: 'If one's intentions and work are good, then privilege, position and recognition come automatically. The whole universe conspires to give back to those who toil for the greater good of humanity.'

3

The Art of Giving and Its Components

Generosity

Generosity, also known as largesse, is the habit of giving without expecting anything in return. It can involve offering time, resources or talents to help someone in need. Often associated with charity as a virtue, generosity is widely regarded as a desirable trait in society. Our timeless customs and traditions influence us in various aspects of life, encouraging us to sacrifice, give or donate for noble causes. Hindu sacred texts are rich with stories that illustrate acts of sacrifice, benevolence and generosity of the highest order. Some of these rare acts of selflessness continue to inspire humankind today.

Hindu mythology is replete with extraordinary instances of people giving away their body parts and wealth in the spirit of daan and *tyaag* (sacrifice). Among them, Dadhichi Rishi's story stands out.

He was entrusted with safeguarding the weapons of the Devas, who were unable to prevent the demons from obtaining them. After a long period, Dadhichi, weary of this responsibility, dissolved the weapons in sacred water and drank it. When the Devas returned and requested their weapons to defeat the demon Vritra, Dadhichi explained that they had become part of his very being. Realizing that his bones were now their only hope, he willingly sacrificed himself in a mystical fire summoned through his austerities.

From his bones, Brahma fashioned powerful weapons, including the 'Vajrayudha', forged from his spine. Infused with divine power, these weapons proved more potent than before, enabling the Devas to triumph over the demons. Dadhichi's supreme sacrifice immortalized his name as an exemplar of selflessness. His bones remain a symbol of India's highest military honour, the Param Vir Chakra, represented as 'Vajra'.

Another rare example is that of King Shibi, renowned for his liberality and selflessness. His story, often cited as a parable of generosity, tells of Agni disguised as a dove and Indra as a hawk. The dove, pursued by the hawk, sought refuge in King Shibi's lap. The hawk, asserting its right to its prey, was countered by the king's offer to compensate it with his own flesh. With King Shibi offering himself up as food, the gods revealed their true identities and blessed him.

Equally inspiring is the tale of Raja Harishchandra, who sacrificed his throne, kingdom, wealth and personal comforts to uphold truth and honour his commitment to Rishi Vishwamitra. His unwavering integrity, tested through great tribulation, remains deeply moving and continues to evoke admiration and nostalgia among believers.

These stories illustrate that the tradition of giving and generosity is deeply rooted in Hindu scriptures and mythology. Mother Teresa beautifully articulated this sentiment: 'It is not how much we give but how much love we put into giving.' This reminds us that mere donation, without compassion and affection, lacks true value. It is the sincerity of giving, not its quantity, that defines its worth.

This is exemplified in a mother's love. A sumptuous meal at a fine restaurant may satisfy hunger, but it cannot compare to food prepared with a mother's affection. That's because the money we pay may buy us food but not affection; love imbued in giving transforms it into a divine act. This is the foundational principle of the Art of Giving too. It is not about material contributions alone but about selfless, heartfelt generosity.

Sir Winston Churchill aptly stated: 'We make a living by what we get. We make a life by what we give.' This profound truth is especially relevant in today's materialistic world, where greed and self-interest often take precedence over compassion. Many people devote their lives to accumulating wealth and securing their children's futures, often at the cost of peace and harmony. In the relentless pursuit of success, we sometimes lose sight of the greater good.

Seeking one's own pleasure and happiness can gradually dry up the spring of divinity in oneself out of sheer ignorance. However, it is a fact of life that many people participate in a rat race to acquire property, power and publicity through all means at their disposal. Surprisingly, despite being educated and well informed, we spare no time to think of the plight of deprived people languishing in distress.

Actually, the pleasure-seeking person will never know that they have been chasing a mirage—the pseudo-pleasure of growing personal wealth, power and luxury. Honestly speaking, is there anything in this world that can give more satisfaction and joy than sacrificing for the greater cause of deprived people? The irony is that giving to the needy, helping people in distress and sacrificing one's own interests for a greater cause gives much greater satisfaction than the very fragile happiness of other forms of pleasure.

Most of us have never experienced the agony of extreme poverty. Millions languish in slums, struggling to secure even two meals a day. They lack access to education, healthcare, and basic dignity. If we dedicate even a fraction of our time and resources to easing their suffering, bringing them hope and a fleeting smile, what greater purpose could life serve? Service to humanity is service to God.

The worth of a person is not measured by what they have done for themselves but by the sacrifices they make for others. The Art of Giving is simply an attitude—to be compassionate and generous towards the destitute and deprived people languishing in the lower rungs of the social order and to help them realize the divinity within themselves. It is, therefore, the endeavour to provide a ray of hope to the weaker and marginalized sections of society as they struggle through life.

To be compassionate to the wounded is really the greatest aspect of humanity; as Steve Maraboli observed in his book *Life, the Truth, and Being Free*: 'A kind gesture can reach a wound that only compassion can heal.' Another eminent author and genius of international repute, Rabindranath Tagore, echoed this sentiment: 'I slept and dreamed that life is all joy. I woke and I saw that life is all service. I served and I saw that service is joy.'

These clearly imply that nothing in this world is better, sweeter, more revered, enticing, delightful and more sacred than service to mankind. Credit should not be given to those who donate a little of their huge possessions because such donations neither affect the donor nor make their life difficult. But when a person makes a sacrifice that causes pain but doesn't complain, it is regarded as a true demonstration of the Art of Giving, which, in essence, has to be selfless. As Kahlil Gibran stated: 'You give but little when you give of your possessions. It is when you give of yourself that you truly give.'

Good Manners and Humility

Delivering kind and gentle words to near and dear ones should be our basic duty. A few words—whether soothing or unkind—can make or break relationships. To establish meaningful connections with others, one has to be articulate, soft-spoken, compassionate and humble. A person's true character is often revealed through their words. One may speak little, but their words should carry weight. Speaking at length is easy; speaking concisely yet meaningfully requires intellect, knowledge, and effective presentation skills. Precision in speech is essential to convey the essence of one's message.

Scathing criticism, harsh remarks and rudeness serve no purpose. Such acts only add salt to the wounds of already distressed people and reflect arrogance. Ultimately, they damage one's own humanity, not the targets of their scorn. One should think carefully before speaking, for once uttered, a bitter word cannot be retracted—just as an arrow released from a bow cannot be taken back.

People should rise above their personal struggles and walk the extra mile to bring smiles to others. Good manners and a warm smile can win hearts and create bonds of goodwill. This, in turn, enables one to reach out and console countless deprived souls suffering in poverty. Showing kindness towards the less fortunate is the first and foremost step in practising the Art of Giving.

Good conduct towards the deprived is an integral part of this philosophy. It is better to remain silent than wound others through harsh words. As the proverb goes, 'speech is silver, silence is golden.' The *Srimad Bhagavad* (Odia version) echoes this sentiment: '*Komala Bachana, Kahi Toshiba Janamana*'—to appease people, one should speak softly and gently.

Appreciation and Gratitude

Appreciation is gratitude in action. It's a fundamental value for building and sustaining human relationships. In today's fast-paced world, we often overlook life's small pleasures. Overburdened and overwhelmed by materialism, we experience stress and burnout, which affects our emotional and physical health across all age groups. Practising appreciation and gratitude in daily life is an art that can be mastered through simple actions. These require little effort but yield tremendous rewards. Human beings crave appreciation and recognition—we all want to feel valued. No one enjoys being criticized. However, not all criticism is unfounded; we must cultivate a positive attitude and learn to appreciate those who care enough to offer constructive feedback.

Ironically, few people take the time to acknowledge goodness when they see it. How often does someone stop to appreciate another? Yet, expressing genuine appreciation works wonders—not only for the person being appreciated but also for the one offering it.

People Are Assets

Most new ideas are delicate and fragile—handle them with care. Most also die prematurely as they are unable to overcome critical barriers. The more important an idea, the greater the resistance it faces. When confronted with unusual suggestions, our first reaction is often to reject them outright. Instead, treat every idea like a baby—nurture it carefully. Out of 10 suggestions, one may prove brilliant enough to transform our lives. The art of appreciation opens our minds to new ideas.

Trust people. When we trust someone, we show appreciation for their efforts. Trust and appreciation energize people, motivating them to do better work. Like watering a sapling, appreciation encourages growth into something greater, ultimately bringing numerous rewards.

Negative people who bring us down can be motivated to change through appreciation. Their negativity often stems from feelings of neglect or the belief that their ideas are always rejected. Acknowledging their worth and respecting their views can yield long-term benefits. Unfortunately, most of us tend to find fault with others rather than appreciate their good qualities. Yet, people are assets; we must learn to recognize their strengths. Everyone has both strong and weak points. By focusing on the good in others, no matter how small, instead of harping on their flaws, we foster friendlier and more compassionate relationships. We should never become fault-finders—nobody is perfect.

The ability to appreciate is a beautiful quality available to everyone, under all circumstances. It includes being thankful for life's little treasures, grateful for the chance to begin each day, and appreciative of the place where karma and divine grace have brought us. Appreciation is life-giving; its absence is destructive. Sadly, in our times, kindness is often overlooked. Good, helpful or loving acts frequently go unnoticed, while shortcomings are swiftly pointed out.

Gratitude is an empowering virtue; its polar opposite—ingratitude—is a reflection of the external ego. At our core, we are pure souls, temporarily inhabiting physical bodies. We must use our God-given free will, guided by love, to make a difference in the world, even in small ways. When each of us contributes in small ways, together, we create a significant impact.

Shishyas (students) should be grateful to their gurus; husbands to their wives, wives to their husbands and both to their children. It's far more effective to praise others and appreciate what we have than to complain about what we lack. Counting our blessings throughout the year greatly enhances the quality of one's life. In fact, appreciation may be one of the most overlooked tools we all have access to.

Cultivating gratitude costs nothing and certainly doesn't require much time, yet its benefits are enormous.

Research reveals that appreciation offers seven key benefits:[1]

- It opens the door to more relationships: Saying 'thank you' is not only good manners but also helps forge new friendships.
- It improves physical health: Grateful people experience fewer aches and pains, and report feeling healthier.
- It improves psychological health: Gratitude reduces toxic emotions, such as envy, resentment, frustration and regret.
- It fosters empathy and reduces aggression: Grateful people display a more pro-social manner, even when others are less kind.
- It promotes better sleep: Maintaining a gratitude journal, noting three things you're grateful for each day, enhances peace of mind and sleep quality.
- It boosts self-esteem: Gratitude increases self-esteem, which is essential for optimal performance.
- It reduces social comparisons and strengthens mental resilience: Gratitude not only reduces stress but also plays a major role in overcoming trauma.

We all have the ability and opportunity to cultivate gratitude. Developing an 'attitude of gratitude' is one of the simplest ways to improve one's satisfaction with life.

---

[1]Morin, Amy, '7 Scientifically Proven Benefits of Gratitude That Will Motivate You to Give Thanks Year-Round', *Forbes*, 23 Nov 2014, www.forbes.com/sites/amymorin/2014/11/23/7-scientifically-proven-benefits-of-gratitude-that-will-motivate-you-to-give-thanks-year-round. Accessed on 21 March 2025.

4

Religion and the Art of Giving

EVERY RELIGION UPHOLDS THE ART OF GIVING AND THE spreading of happiness and peace—principles that inspired me during my struggles to persevere and move ahead in life. There is nothing novel about the Art of Giving or kindness; they are deeply embedded in all religions.

Giving material goods is just one form of generosity. One can always extend the spirit of giving into their behaviour by embracing kindness, empathy and selflessness. At its core, the Art of Giving springs from a heart that expects nothing in return. It finds its essence in the pure joy of giving, advocating for simple living and bringing smiles to the faces of those who need it most—irrespective of class, creed, sex, place of origin, race or any other form of stratification. Givers experience immense joy when they can alleviate suffering, especially when their acts are free of obligation or compulsion.

In various religious teachings, such as in Indian scriptures, charity, or daan, holds a place of great prominence. The act of giving carries profound significance across the world's major religions, each offering unique teachings and practices that highlight the transformative power of generosity. The Art of Giving exemplifies selflessness and its positive impact on society, demonstrating that life's greatest joys come from giving and sharing with others.

In Christianity, the call to embody Christ's love through acts of kindness serves as a beacon of hope and compassion, urging believers to extend forgiveness and love as they have received from God. This is reflected in the Bible's teachings, where kindness, compassion and selfless acts are central tenets of a faithful life.

Islam, with its deeply rooted principles of charity and compassion, emphasizes the importance of helping those in need through various forms of giving, such as zakat—an obligatory form of almsgiving—and sadaqah, or voluntary acts of charity. These practices promote social welfare and support for the underprivileged, reflecting a commitment to justice and communal responsibility.

Judaism's concept of tzedakah underscores the pursuit of social justice, encouraging acts of giving performed with empathy and respect. Rooted in the Hebrew Bible and further elaborated by scholars like Maimonides, tzedakah goes beyond mere charity to include kindness and justice that uplift the community.

Buddhism's practice of *dana*, or generosity, is foundational to the path of enlightenment, promoting selflessness and the relinquishment of attachments. Dana is considered a vital practice that fosters ethical behaviour, mental calmness and insight, ultimately leading to spiritual liberation.

Confucianism, while not traditionally categorized as a religion, places significant emphasis on the virtues of *ren* (benevolence) and *yi* (righteousness), advocating giving that is rooted in compassion and moral duty. Confucian teachings stress empathy, reciprocity and the moral obligation to care for others, creating a harmonious and ethical society.

This exploration of the Art of Giving across different religious traditions reveals a shared understanding that generosity is not merely a transactional act but a deeply spiritual practice that fosters empathy, enhances moral development and contributes to the betterment of society.

HINDUISM

Hinduism, one of the world's oldest religions, is rich with teachings and practices that emphasize giving, kindness, charity and compassion. These principles are woven into the fabric of Hindu philosophy, stories and rituals, encouraging adherents to lead lives that are not only spiritually fulfilling but also socially responsible. This section explores the various facets of giving in Hinduism, examining scriptural teachings, mythological stories, and modern practices that illustrate the profound impact of these values on individuals and society.

As mentioned before, daan occupies a place of great prominence in Hinduism. Helping those in need is the very essence of daan. It may involve giving food to the hungry or imparting knowledge of the Vedas—these are considered the highest forms of daan. When a hungry man comes to one's door, he is regarded as a guest in the form of *deva* or God.

In India, there are many stories of families choosing to starve rather than turn away a beggar. Religious scriptures advocate charity not merely as an act of altruism but as a moral obligation for the upliftment of humanity. They encourage compassion and sensitivity towards human suffering and social injustice, promoting social service, global brotherhood and respect for universal human values.

In the *Mahabharata*, the section titled 'Dana-dharma Parva' offers detailed instructions on philanthropy. One of the most celebrated examples of charity in Hindu mythology is the story of Karna. Despite knowing it would weaken him in battle, Karna gives away his divine armour and earrings—which could have saved him from death—to Indra, the King of Gods, who comes disguised as a Brahmin. This act of supreme generosity underscores the importance of selfless giving.

The *Bhagavad Gita* highlights how *yajna* (sacrificial offerings), daan, knowledge and understanding enable one to develop purity of heart and a sense of righteous achievement. Shankaracharya, in the eighth century, spoke of 'danam sam vibhagah'—the righteous distribution of resources.

The *Ramayana* portrays Rama's selflessness in abdicating the throne in favour of Bharata, symbolizing the sacrifice of personal gain for the greater good. The *Dharmasutras* contain elaborate descriptions of charity, highlighting philanthropic principles that advocate generosity, fairness and the responsibility of the privileged towards the less fortunate.

Roots of Dharma

Compassion and kindness are integral qualities rooted in the principles of dharma, emphasizing the importance of serving others. The foundational elements of dharma are highlighted in the *Vayu Purana*: *Adroha* (absence of ill-feeling), *alobha* (absence of covetousness), *dama* (self-control), *bhutadaya* (kindness to living beings), *tapas* (penance), *brahmacharya* (celibacy), *satya* (truthfulness), *anukrosa* (compassion and tenderness), *kshama* (forgiveness) and *dhriti* (fortitude) are considered the roots of dharma, though they are challenging to fully embody.

—*Vayu Purana* I.57.116

Shishtachara and Sympathy

Expressing sympathy towards others is an essential aspect of polite behaviour or shishtachara. The *Vayu Purana* outlines eight characteristics of this principle: charity, truthfulness, penance, the absence of greed, learning, sacrifice, procreation and sympathy.

—*Vayu Purana* I.59.37

Compassion for the Afflicted

True spiritual merit is intertwined with one's ability to sympathize with the afflicted. A Brahmana may be serene and even-tempered, but if he lacks empathy for those who suffer, the virtues of his austerity are lost, akin to water kept in a broken pot.

—*Shrimad Bhagavata Purana* IV.14.41

Service to All Beings

God resides within all beings as their innermost soul. Ignoring this divine presence in others while making a show of worship through images is futile. True worship involves recognizing God in all beings and serving them with love, gifts and honour. Service rendered to others is essentially service to God, fostering a sense of unity and reducing the fear of death and self-interest deprivation.

—*Shrimad Bhagavata Purana* III.29.21-27

Helping the Needy

In the *Mahabharata*, Bhishma teaches that one's desires for oneself should be mirrored in one's desires for others. The surplus wealth one accumulates should be used to alleviate the needs of the less fortunate. This practice of wealth management through trade or investment is ordained by the Creator to ensure the well-being of all.

—*Mahabharata*, 'Santi Parva', Section CCLIX

FORGIVENESS AND KINDNESS IN HINDU STORIES

In Hindu mythology, gods are often portrayed as forgiving and compassionate. These stories hold profound moral significance, teaching people to live virtuous lives.

Lord Shiva's Boundless Mercy

In Hindu belief, Lord Shiva is revered for his endless compassion, a key aspect of his role as the God of Destruction who paves the way for new beginnings. Shiva, one of the Trimurti alongside Brahma the Creator and Vishnu the Preserver, exemplifies this virtue. His compassion is crucial for maintaining universal balance—he destroys not for the sake of destruction but to enable growth and spiritual renewal.

Followers of Shiva find solace in his mercy, believing it aids them in correcting their mistakes and ultimately attaining *moksha* (liberation). His compassion is not merely a narrative; it aligns with the cyclical worldview of Hinduism, symbolizing the natural cycle of life, death and rebirth.

Lord Krishna's Teachings on Forgiveness

The teachings of Lord Krishna also embody a profound understanding of forgiveness, underscoring its importance for personal and spiritual development. In the *Mahabharata*, Krishna imparts wisdom from the *Bhagavad Gita* to Arjuna, focusing on duty, righteousness and compassion. His philosophy of forgiveness is analytical—he warns that harbouring ill will disrupts one's dharma.

Krishna encourages releasing anger and practising understanding, leading to inner peace and societal harmony.

According to him, forgiveness is a strength, not a weakness—it fosters resilience and promotes inclusivity in society.

The Compassionate Mother Goddess

In Hinduism, the Mother Goddess is celebrated for her unconditional compassion and kindness. Like a loving mother, she forgives her children unconditionally. Goddesses such as Parvati, Durga and Kali embody different aspects of maternal love and forgiveness.

Devotees admire these goddesses not only for their power and bravery but also for their willingness to forgive, symbolizing the transformative power of forgiveness. This maternal grace provides comfort and hope to individuals, encouraging renewal and self-improvement.

For example, devotees who seek forgiveness from the goddess after making mistakes often feel granted a second chance to redeem themselves. This mirrors human interactions, where empathy and second chances allow for personal growth.

Lord Rama's Virtue of Pardon

In the Ramayana, Lord Rama is celebrated for his capacity to forgive—showing kindness to both friends and foes. Rama's forgiveness extends even to those who wrong him, demonstrating his moral strength and justice.

For instance, despite Ravana's abduction of Sita, Rama honours Ravana's valour in battle. His respect for his adversary demonstrates the ability to forgive and respect even in conflict. Rama's forgiving nature highlights the importance of reflection over reaction, inspiring us to choose empathy in our own lives.

Sage Narada and Divine Clemency

Sage Narada, a divine messenger between gods and humans, is known for his kindness and wisdom in promoting forgiveness. Narada's interventions often resolve conflicts and foster understanding and mercy.

His compassionate guidance reflects the divine value of forgiveness in Hinduism, illustrating that forgiving others is as sacred as any ritual or prayer.

ANECDOTES OF KINDNESS AND COMPASSION

The Tale of Rantideva

Rantideva, a king renowned for his immense generosity, is a profound example from Hindu mythology. According to the *Shrimad Bhagavata Purana*, Rantideva chose to suffer hunger and thirst himself rather than allow any guest to go without food or water. His compassion and selflessness were so great that he even offered his own share of water to a thirsty visitor, epitomizing the ideal of dana.

Annapurna Devi

The goddess Annapurna, considered the Hindu deity of nourishment, symbolizes the importance of food donation. Temples dedicated to Annapurna in India often engage in large-scale food distribution, ensuring that no devotee leaves hungry. This practice highlights the belief that feeding the hungry is one of the highest forms of charity.

Dharma of the *Mahabharata*

The *Mahabharata* contains numerous lessons on the importance of charity. In addition to Karna, the story of Yudhishthira illustrates the virtue of dana. Known for his righteousness, Yudhishthira performed the *Rajasuya Yajna*, distributing immense wealth to the people, thereby underscoring the importance of sharing one's prosperity.

The Generosity of Tamil Kings

The Tamil kings, especially from the Chola and Pandya dynasties, were known for their patronage of arts, culture and public welfare. They built extensive irrigation systems, temples and educational institutions, demonstrating the Hindu principle of dana through state policies and personal acts of generosity.

Environmental Stewardship in Hinduism

Hinduism's teachings extend compassion to the environment as well. The principle of *ahimsa* (non-violence) is not limited to human beings but includes all living creatures and nature. The sacredness of rivers, trees and animals in Hindu tradition encourages environmental conservation and protection as acts of kindness and responsibility.

Charity as a Duty in Hinduism

In Hindu culture, acts of charity and giving are viewed as duties rather than mere acts of kindness. The practice of giving is believed to begin within one's family but extends beyond the household.

The primary responsibility within the family is to ensure the well-being of its members and meet their needs. It is believed that wealth acquired by an individual is meant not just for personal benefit but also for the welfare of the extended family and community. An example of familial charity in Hindu tradition involves caring for relatives facing challenges. One is encouraged to make sacrifices, even forsaking personal ambitions, for the sake of family unity.

Giving in Hinduism extends beyond material possessions— it also encompasses sacrificing dreams and aspirations when necessary for the greater good of all stakeholders. The focus remains on benefiting the collective rather than prioritizing personal desires.

Anna Dana: The Charity of Food

While charity starts within the family circle, Hindus are encouraged to extend their generosity beyond familial boundaries. One significant practice is *anna dana* (food donation). This tradition emphasizes the importance of sharing food with visitors and those in need.

According to custom, homeowners should not eat until they have offered food to their dependents, deities, ancestors and beggars or the needy. Before each meal, it is customary for the homeowner to stand outside and invite anyone in need to join them. This invitation is extended three times before the family partakes in the meal, either alone or with any guest who accepts the offer.

Generosity in Contemporary India

In modern India, these ancient principles continue to inspire acts of philanthropy and social service.

Many Hindu temples run *annadanam* programmes, providing free meals to thousands of devotees and the needy. The Siddhivinayak Temple in Mumbai and the Tirupati Balaji Temple in Andhra Pradesh are notable examples of institutions that engage in extensive charitable activities, including education, healthcare and disaster relief.

The tradition of guru dakshina (offering gifts to teachers) also continues to flourish. This practice, rooted in the principle of giving, serves as a mark of respect and gratitude towards teachers. It not only honours the teacher-student relationship but also reinforces the value of selfless giving and humility.

The principles of giving, kindness, charity and compassion are integral to Hinduism, deeply embedded in its scriptures, stories, and rituals. These values not only shape personal conduct but also foster a sense of social responsibility and community welfare. By drawing from ancient teachings and adapting them to contemporary contexts, Hindus around the world continue to promote a culture of generosity and empathy.

As these practices evolve, they reinforce the timeless message that true fulfilment and societal harmony are achieved through selfless service and the upliftment of others. This exploration of Hinduism's emphasis on giving and compassion illustrates how these enduring principles remain relevant and impactful in the modern world. Through a combination of scriptural teachings, mythological stories, and contemporary examples, it is evident that the Art of Giving in Hinduism is a profound and lasting legacy that continues to inspire individuals and communities to lead lives of service, kindness and compassion.

Continuation of beauty is more important than the creation of beauty.

SIKHISM AND THE PRINCIPLE OF GIVING

Founded about 500 years ago in Punjab, Sikhism is the

world's fifth-largest religion. The faith is distinguished by its profound commitment to *seva* (service), a principle deeply ingrained in its followers. Sikhism promotes giving, kindness, charity and compassion through its teachings and practices. Guru Nanak, the founder of Sikhism, taught that God resides within all individuals, making serving others equivalent to serving God. This principle is foundational in Sikhism, encouraging followers to lead compassionate lives integrated with the larger society.

Seva, or selfless service, is a central tenet of the Sikh faith, urging Sikhs to help others without any expectation of personal gain. This practice is viewed as a path to draw closer to God and cultivate humility.

Gurdwaras, Sikh places of worship, are not just for prayer but also serve as community centres, soup kitchens and shelters. The concept of *langar* involves providing free meals to people of all backgrounds, emphasizing equality and community spirit. This tradition continues robustly today, with gurdwaras worldwide serving millions of free meals annually.

The history of Sikhism is replete with examples of selfless service and sacrifice. The Sikh gurus themselves set powerful examples of giving and compassion. Guru Amar Das established the tradition of langar, where everyone— regardless of caste, creed or social status—could eat together as equals. Guru Hargobind, the sixth guru, founded hospitals and cared for the sick and needy, demonstrating the faith's commitment to welfare.

The Psychological and Spiritual Benefits of Giving

Studies indicate that shifting focus from personal problems to helping others can significantly improve mental health. Acts of giving are associated with lower blood pressure, reduced mortality rates, better moods and increased happiness.

In Sikhism, seva also serves as a form of meditation, providing a sense of purpose and tranquillity. This practice aligns with the Sikh principles of:

- *Sarbat da bhala*: Seeking the welfare of all
- *Chardi kala*: Maintaining eternal positivity

The Philosophy of Seva in Sikhism

Sikh teachings emphasize three types of seva:

- *Taan* (physical service): Involves hands-on activities, such as participating in langar, cooking and serving meals, cleaning gurdwaras and providing physical assistance to those in need.
- *Maan* (Intellectual and emotional service): Includes offering one's talents, such as teaching and mentoring; and providing empathy and emotional support to those in distress.
- *Dhan* (Material service): Involving charitable acts and philanthropy performed without seeking recognition. This includes donating money, resources and goods to those in need, supporting community projects and funding charitable initiatives.

Seva in Daily Sikh Life

Seva is integral to daily life for Sikhs. Each day, Sikhs repeat a prayer called the *Ardas*, where they invoke Sarbat da bhala— meaning 'blessings for everyone'.

Sikh Humanitarian Efforts

Sikh volunteers have been at the forefront of humanitarian efforts globally:

- During the Rohingya crisis in Myanmar, Sikhs provided essential aid to refugees.
- In the aftermath of the Paris terror attacks, Sikh communities offered support and assistance to those affected.
- During the farmers' protests in India, Sikhs organized langars to feed not only the protesters but also the police, showcasing their commitment to service and unity.

Seva during the COVID-19 Pandemic

During the COVID-19 pandemic, Sikh communities worldwide initiated relief efforts:

- Oxygen langars to provide free oxygen to those in need.
- In Maharashtra, a gurdwara fed two million people in 10 weeks.
- Some Sikh gurdwaras also melted gold collected over decades to set up hospitals and medical colleges during the second wave.

Sikh Beliefs and Community Service

The Sikh holy book, the Guru Granth Sahib, states: 'You become like the one you serve.'

This underscores the belief that to become one with God, one must serve others. This teaching is central to Sikhism, inspiring followers to engage in acts of kindness and charity.

Sikhism's emphasis on giving, kindness, charity and compassion is deeply rooted in its teachings and traditions. The principle of seva, as taught by Guru Nanak and enshrined in the Guru Granth Sahib, continues to inspire Sikhs to lead lives of selfless service and community support. Through historical examples and contemporary practices, the transformative power of giving is evident, fostering a spirit of equality, compassion and harmony.

Sikhism's commitment to service enriches the lives of its followers and contributes to the well-being of humanity, demonstrating that true spirituality lies in uplifting and serving others.

CHRISTIANITY

In a world often marked by challenges and uncertainties, the call to embody Christ's love through acts of kindness stands as a beacon of hope and compassion for Christians. Rooted in biblical teachings, kindness carries profound significance, transcending mere gestures. The Bible is replete with verses emphasizing the importance of kindness and love.

Ephesians 4:32 urges believers to 'be kind to one another, tenderhearted, forgiving one another, as God in Christ forgave you.' This verse sets the foundation for understanding that our acts of kindness are an extension of the forgiveness and love we have received from God.

Kindness involves being considerate, compassionate and generous towards others. It is a selfless and empathetic approach to interactions, characterized by acts of goodwill, empathy and understanding. The aim is to alleviate others' burdens or bring joy without expecting anything in return.

True kindness stems from a genuine desire to contribute positively to someone's well-being—whether the person is known or a stranger. Authentic kindness arises from a selfless place, driven by empathy and genuine concern for the welfare of others. Acts lacking sincerity or driven by personal gain do not embody true kindness. Furthermore, actions that cause harm or disregard others' feelings cannot be considered kind.

Biblical Examples of Kindness

The Bible showcases numerous figures who exemplified kindness and compassion through their actions.

Jesus: The epitome of kindness, Jesus consistently showed compassion, healed the sick and offered forgiveness to those in need.

The Good Samaritan: According to a parable, a Samaritan demonstrated profound kindness by helping a wounded stranger on the road when others passed by.

Ruth: Her loyalty and devotion to her mother-in-law, Naomi, displayed deep kindness and compassion.

Boaz: He showed kindness to Ruth by allowing her to glean in his fields and providing extra food for her and Naomi.

Joseph: Despite facing betrayal, Joseph displayed kindness towards his brothers by eventually forgiving and reconciling with them.

Tabitha: Known for her acts of kindness and charity, she was resurrected by the apostle Peter due to the impact of her benevolent deeds.

Acts of Kindness

Central to the Christian faith is the call to imitate Christ and live a life that mirrors His character. In John 13:34–35,

Jesus says, 'A new command I give you: Love one another. As I have loved you, so you must love one another. By this, everyone will know that you are my disciples if you love one another.'

Acts of kindness, driven by selfless love, become a visible expression of discipleship and a testament to the transformative power of Christ's love. It has various components:

Random Acts: Surprise others with unexpected generosity and show love without expecting anything in return, mirroring God's unconditional love for humanity.

Forgiveness: Extend forgiveness to those who have wronged you, as Christ forgave us. This fosters reconciliation, healing, and cultivates humility, recognizing that all people are created in God's image and worthy of love and respect.

Loving the Unlovable: Demonstrate empathy and compassion towards those whom society often rejects, just as God is compassionate towards all of His creation. This inclusive love can transform lives and spread Christ's message.

Charitable Giving: Give to those in need and engage in acts of service and kindness, mirroring God's desire for His followers to serve one another. This echoes God's love for the marginalized and downtrodden.

Words of Encouragement: Offer uplifting words of kindness and encouragement. Share the message of God's love and salvation, contributing to the spiritual well-being of others.

Acts of Kindness as a Witness

Acts of kindness become a powerful witness to the world. In Matthew 5:16, Jesus encourages believers to 'let your light shine before others, that they may see your good deeds and glorify your Father in heaven.'

Kindness transcends barriers and societal expectations, drawing people closer to God through the genuine care and compassion demonstrated by believers. Acts of kindness reflect God's love, reminding us of the foundation of our faith and the boundless love that sustains us. This impact shapes every aspect of a believer's life, influencing thoughts, actions and relationships. By embodying Christ's love, Christians acknowledge His unconditional and sacrificial nature as the cornerstone of their faith. Reflecting on God's love catalyses spiritual growth, encouraging believers to emulate His character and develop a Christ-like mindset. It reinforces our identity as children of God and inspires us to live righteously, especially during difficult times. Regular reflection deepens our intimacy with God, fostering a closer connection and a clearer understanding of His will.

The Christian Principle of Giving

At the core of Christianity lies the principle of giving. John 3:16 beautifully encapsulates this: 'For God so loved the world, He gave...'

We embody God's nature most profoundly when we give. Jesus himself said, 'I did not come to be served, but to serve, and to give my life' (Matthew 20:28). While the world urges us to acquire as much as we can, to truly emulate Jesus, we must learn to give.

Giving Begins with a Cause: The disciples of Jesus exemplified this by abandoning everything—their homes, jobs and security to follow him. Their sacrifices stemmed from being captivated by a profound cause—the imminent Kingdom of God and the presence of the Son of God among them. They longed to be part of a transformative mission.

This spirit of sacrifice continued beyond the first followers of Jesus. The Book of Acts highlights men and women who willingly gave up their possessions, livelihoods and time for Christ. They faced persecution, martyrdom and suffering, yet they persevered because they identified with a greater purpose. These early Christians recognized that giving was vital for building God's Kingdom. By contributing what they could, they actively participated in its expansion on earth.

We can choose a life of selfishness, exist without purpose, and ultimately fade away, or we can dedicate ourselves to the noble cause of reaching people for Christ, thereby discovering true life.

Giving entails a sacrifice: Jesus stated, 'Just as the Son of Man did not come to be served, but to serve, and to give his life as a ransom for many' (Matthew 20:28). Godly giving inherently involves sacrifice, and He certainly expects this commitment from us.

One profound moment came when Jesus observed people making their contributions to the temple. While many gave substantial amounts, a widow came forward and offered two coins, worth less than a cent. Jesus highlighted her act to teach His disciples that the value of a gift is less important than the sacrifice it represents. The widow had the option to keep one coin, but she chose to give everything she had, holding nothing back. This illustrates a key tenet of Christianity: we have not truly given to God until we have given everything.

Florence Nightingale once wrote in her diary, 'I am 30 years of age, the age at which Christ began His mission. Now no more childish things, no more vain things. Now, Lord, let me think only of Thy will.' Years later, as she reflected on her remarkable life, she was asked for her secret. She simply replied, 'I have kept nothing back from God.'

Giving leads to life: In the Holy Land, a brook flows into the Sea of Galilee, renowned for its abundant fish. This body of water then channels into the Jordan River, which nurtures the surrounding desert, transforming it into a fertile land of milk and honey. Eventually, the Jordan River reaches the Dead Sea, a unique body of water with no outlet. While it absorbs water, its high salinity makes it lifeless. This serves as a powerful metaphor: to thrive, one must be willing to give. Jesus taught, 'Give, and it will be given to you.'

As Karl Menninger observed, 'Our capacity to give is one of the best indications of mental health; few generous individuals struggle with mental illness.' Therefore, a fulfilling life begins with the act of giving.

Giving produces joy: People give not because it hurts, but because it brings joy. Jesus stated, 'It is more blessed to give than to receive' (Acts 20:35). The happiest individuals are those who embrace the joy of giving.

Author Thomas Carlyle recalls a childhood experience when a beggar came to his door—he impulsively broke into his savings bank and gave everything he had. He described it as the most profound joy he had ever felt.

The essence of Christianity lies in giving. It begins with a cause, involves sacrifice, leads to life, and ultimately brings joy. Through giving, we reflect God's love and embody the core of our faith.

For Christians, the foundation of charity is rooted in the Hebrew Bible's teachings. In the New Testament, Jesus's parables and actions further emphasize the importance of charitable sentiments.

ISLAM

The word 'charity' appears many times in the Holy Quran, emphasizing acts of kindness and helping those in need, such as supporting orphans and widows. Charity holds a significant place in Islam, supported by examples and anecdotes from Islamic teachings.

The concept of giving in Islam is deeply rooted in the teachings of the Quran and the Hadith, reflecting a multifaceted approach to charity and generosity. These principles highlight the profound impact of giving on both individual and societal levels, promoting a balanced and compassionate community.

Abu Bakr, the first Caliph, was known for his immense generosity. He once gave all his wealth to support the Muslim community. When asked what he had left for his family, he replied, 'Allah and His Messenger.'

Forms of Charity in Islam

There are several forms of giving in Islam, each with its unique purpose and application:

Zakat: An obligatory almsgiving that acts as a social welfare system, ensuring the redistribution of wealth to the needy. It contributes to the socio-economic balance of society.

Sadaqah: A voluntary act of charity that can be given at any time and in any amount, often aimed at helping the underprivileged.

Hibah: A freely given gift, which can be directed to anyone, including non-Muslims and the affluent.

Waqf: An endowment of property or assets for charitable purposes, which is irrevocable and perpetual.

Al-Wasiyyah: A will or bequest that takes effect after the death of the testator, often used to continue charitable contributions posthumously.

Motivations for Giving in Islam

Islamic teachings promote giving through various motivations:

- **Targhib (Reward):** Encouragement through the promise of rewards in the Hereafter for generous giving.
  Example: 'The example of those who spend their wealth in the way of Allah is like a seed [of grain] that sprouts seven ears; in every ear, there are a hundred grains.'
  —Quran 2:261
- **Tarhib (Fear):** The fear of punishment for neglecting obligatory charity, such as zakat.
  Example: 'And let not those who [greedily] withhold what Allah has given them of His bounty ever think that it is better for them. Rather, it is worse for them.'
  —Quran 3:180
- **Ihsan (Altruism):** Performing acts of charity out of pure love and servitude to Allah. This is done without the expectation of rewards or fear of punishment.
- Example: The story of Sa'id bin Amir, who distributed a substantial monetary gift to the needy instead of using it for his own comfort.
- **Ikhwah (Brotherhood):** A strong sense of community and belonging motivates individuals to support one another.
  Example: The Ansar of Medina shared their wealth and homes with the Muhajirun during the early days of Islam.

Allah's guidance helps believers stay on the right path, remain humble, and care for others as they do for themselves and their loved ones. Allah has given humans hearts to feel compassion, but it is both the heart and mind that make people truly good human beings. Helping others is a fundamental act of humanity.

The Prophet Muhammad (PBUH) also said, 'None of you truly believes until he loves for his brother what he loves for himself' (*Sahih al-Bukhari*).

The Importance of Giving to Others

Inequality and poverty cause hardship in many communities. In Islam, wealth is a gift from Allah, and those who are financially stable are tested by whether they share their wealth with others. As our wealth is a gift from Him, it can be taken away by Him too.

The Prophet Muhammad (PBUH) was known for his generosity. He once said, 'The upper hand is better than the lower hand'—he who gives in charity is better than he who takes it (*Sahih al-Bukhari*).

The Prophet's life was filled with instances of giving. He often gave away his personal belongings to those in need, even if it meant he had to go without. On one occasion, a man came to the Prophet asking for charity. Although he had nothing to give at that moment, the Prophet instructed the man to buy something on credit and promised to pay the debt later. This action reflects the Prophet's commitment to helping others, even through personal sacrifice.

Charity in Times of Crisis

When Arabia experienced a severe famine, Caliph Umar ibn al-Khattab initiated a massive relief operation, providing food and resources to the affected areas. This demonstrated the Islamic principle of collective responsibility in times of crisis.

During the Battle of Tabuk, The Prophet (PBUH) called upon the Muslims to donate generously to support the expedition. Uthman ibn Affan, a wealthy companion, donated a large amount of money, significantly helping to equip the army. The Prophet (PBUH) praised Uthman's generosity, saying, 'Nothing will harm Uthman after today, no matter what he does.'

Ramadan Charity

Though charitable acts are encouraged year-round, they hold special importance during Ramadan. Ibn Abbas reported: 'The Prophet was the most generous of all the people, and he used to become more generous in Ramadan when Gabriel met him. Gabriel used to meet him every night during Ramadan to revise the Quran with him. Allah's Messenger then used to be more generous than the fast wind' (*Sahih al-Bukhari*).

Fasting is a key part of Ramadan, but some people, such as those with long-term illnesses or pregnant women, cannot fast. Instead, they make a monetary donation known as *fidya*, which equals the cost of feeding one person for a day.

Why Is Charity Important?

The Holy Prophet (PBUH) said, 'The believer's shade on the Day of Judgement will be his charitable acts' (*Tirmidhi*). Giving reminds us that everything we have is temporary and belongs to Allah. By giving in charity, we follow the Prophet's example and help lift those around us.

In one instance, a woman came to Aisha, the wife of the Prophet (PBUH), with her two daughters. Aisha gave her three dates. The woman gave one date to each of her daughters and kept one for herself. The daughters, however, ate their dates quickly and looked at their mother with pleading eyes. The mother then split her own date into two halves and gave one half to each daughter. Aisha was deeply moved by this act of selflessness and compassion. When the Prophet (PBUH) heard of this, he said, 'Allah has guaranteed Paradise for her because of this act' (*Sahih Muslim*).

One should never forget the importance of charity in Islam. One's acts of kindness not only benefit others but also elevate their own spiritual journey. By giving, we embody the spirit of Islam and follow the example of the Prophet Muhammad (PBUH) and his companions.

Sadaqah

Sadaqah, a voluntary act of charity, is given purely to please Allah (SWT) without expecting anything in return. The word means 'righteousness' and derives from *sidq*, meaning sincerity. It reflects genuine faith and good character, fostering a compassionate and just society.

The Quran and Sunnah stress the importance of regular sadaqah, promising numerous benefits to those who give:

- Sadaqah fulfils one's needs. While people often save for their future, they are reminded that Allah is the true provider. By helping others, they trust in Allah's promise of provision.
- Sadaqah eases hardships and wards off calamities. The Prophet Muhammad (PBUH) said, 'Give sadaqah without delay, for it stands in the way of calamity' (*Tirmidhi*). Giving during times of struggle demonstrates strong faith and gratitude.
- Sadaqah is an investment in this life and the

Hereafter. Allah promises to increase the wealth and success of those who give, making charity a spiritual and worldly investment.

- Sadaqah erases sins. The Prophet (PBUH) said, 'Charity extinguishes sins like water extinguishes fire' (*Ibn Majah*). Even a small, sincere donation can atone for sins.

- Sadaqah leads to Jannah. One of the eight gates of Jannah is called 'Baab As-Sadaqah', reserved for those who frequently give in charity. Helping orphans, widows and the poor can lead one to this blessed gate.

- Sadaqah will be a shield on the Day of Judgement. The Prophet (PBUH) said, 'The believer's shade on the Day of Resurrection will be his charity' (*Tirmidhi*). Acts of kindness will bring comfort and protection on that day.

- Sadaqah purifies the soul. Spending in the way of Allah cleanses the heart of greed and strengthens righteousness.

- Sadaqah increases the likelihood of accepted duas. The story of the three men trapped in a cave demonstrates how Allah responded to their sincere good deeds and saved them, showing the power of charitable acts in having duas answered.

- Sadaqah brings balance to society. It reduces poverty, supports the vulnerable and fosters a sense of social responsibility. The Prophet (PBUH) said, 'Your smile for your brother is a charity. Removing stones, thorns, or bones from paths is a charity. Guiding a lost person is a charity' (*Sahih al-Bukhari*). These simple yet meaningful acts of kindness reflect the broad scope of charity in Islam.

- Sadaqah Jariyah, or continuous charity, earns ongoing

rewards even after death. The Prophet (PBUH) said, 'When a man dies, his deeds end except for three: Sadaqah Jariyah, beneficial knowledge, or a virtuous descendant who prays for him' (*Sahih Muslim*). Building a well, funding education, or supporting a medical facility are examples of Sadaqah Jariyah that continue to benefit others and earn blessings long after one's passing.

Through acts of charity, Muslims emulate the Prophet's compassion, support the needy and strengthen their spiritual bond with Allah. By giving regularly and selflessly, they enrich their own lives and contribute to a more just and merciful society, both in this world and the next.

JUDAISM

'The world endures because of three activities: study of Torah, divine worship, and deeds of loving-kindness.'

—*Sefer HaAggadah*

In Hebrew, the closest word to 'philanthropy' is tzedakah. Though often used interchangeably with charity, tzedakah is more accurately a form of social justice. It benefits not only the recipients but also the donors and those who facilitate the support. Like justice, tzedakah is not something done to someone—it is done with someone. In Hebrew, the word for 'to give' is *natan*, which, in both Hebrew and English, is a palindrome, readable forward and backward. This reflects the reciprocal nature of tzedakah: giving is also receiving. More than a financial transaction, it builds trusting relationships and honours the contributions of time, effort and insight.

A *mitzvah* is one of the 613 commandments Jews are obligated to observe. More broadly, it refers to any good deed. The mitzvah of tzedakah is among the most important. Traditionally, most Jewish homes had a blue-and-white tin box for depositing tzedakah coins, instilling from childhood the responsibility to care for fellow Jews in need. Though today's methods of giving are more complex, the motivation remains the same: to sustain the Jewish people, enhance Jewish life, and strengthen the community for the present and future. During daily prayer services, a *pushke* (charity box) is often passed around, signifying the connection between prayer and charity.

At the end of every Jewish worship service, the *Aleinu* prayer expresses the Jewish people's aspiration to 'perfect the world under the sovereignty of God.' This concept, known as *tikkun olam* (repairing the world), embodies the commitment to social justice. The Torah declares, 'There will never cease to be needy ones in your land' (Deuteronomy 15:11), highlighting the perpetual need for compassion and generosity.

In ancient times, when the Torah governed an agricultural society, tzedakah was expressed through practices such as leaving the corners of fields unharvested so the poor could gather food. As economies diversified, rabbis redefined tzedakah in financial terms, creating public and private funds to support the needy. Food banks and soup kitchens were established long before government welfare systems existed. The sages viewed social welfare not as charity but as a matter of economic and social justice.

During the medieval period, Rabbi Moshe ben Maimon, also known as Maimonides, codified tzedakah laws, introducing an eight-stage hierarchy of giving. He taught that the highest form of tzedakah enables recipients to become self-sufficient. His approach continues to shape

Jewish philanthropy today, prompting ongoing reflection on how much to give and whether giving should be anonymous.

The Meaning and Practice of Tzedakah

Tzedakah is more than giving money—it is an expression of compassion and empathy. Maimonides wrote, 'Whoever gives tzedakah to the poor with a sour expression and in a surly manner, even if he gives a thousand gold pieces, loses his merit. One should instead give cheerfully and joyfully and empathize with the recipient's sorrow.' True tzedakah involves both the hand and heart: the act of giving is accompanied by kindness and respect. The donor should give with a pleasant demeanour and a full heart, ensuring the recipient is not made to feel ashamed or rebuked.

Jewish tradition teaches that tzedakah benefits the giver as much as, if not more than, the recipient. While the poor receive material support, the donor earns the merit of participating in divine work. The act of giving is thus spiritually enriching, forging a deeper connection with God.

The Four Stages of Giving

There are four stages of giving: minimum, good, better and best.

- **Minimum:** The smallest annual contribution is an amount under $2. However, for a person with adequate means, this is considered unacceptably low.
- **Good:** The appropriate contribution for someone of sufficient means is 10 per cent of their net income.
- **Better:** Giving 20 per cent of net income is viewed as a more virtuous act of tzedakah. However, the rabbis cautioned against extreme generosity that could lead the donor to financial hardship. Exceptions to

this limit include cases such as ransoming captives, saving lives, supporting Torah scholars or seeking atonement for sins.

- **Best:** The highest form of tzedakah is collective responsibility, in which the community ensures the needs of the poor are met. Each person of adequate means is expected to give their fair share, determined voluntarily or by the community. The obligation to provide for the poor falls on the community as a whole rather than on individuals alone. Individuals are, however, responsible for advocating on behalf of those in need.

Unlike traditional communal tzedakah, contemporary Jewish philanthropy is often practised privately, with individuals determining the amount they give. Nonetheless, the principles of justice, empathy and dignity that define tzedakah remain timeless.

BUDDHISM

'If beings knew, as I know, the results of giving and sharing, they would not eat without having given, nor would the stain of selfishness overcome their minds. Even if it were their last bite, their last mouthful, they would not eat without having shared, if there were someone to receive their gift.'

—*Itivuttaka* 26

The practice of giving, known as 'dana' in Pali, holds a place of pre-eminence in the Buddha's teachings. It refers both to the act of giving and the donation itself. The Buddha used the word *caga* to describe the inner virtue of generosity that connects dana to the spiritual path. This term is significant, as it also means relinquishment or renunciation. True generosity requires giving more than what is expected or customary, relative to one's resources and circumstances. It involves relinquishing not only material possessions but also stinginess, clinging and greed. In this way, generosity becomes an act of selflessness—a giving of oneself.

The Buddha emphasized that the spiritual merit of a gift depends not on its size but on the attitude with which it is given. A small donation that requires personal sacrifice is of greater spiritual value than a large but insignificant gift from a wealthy person. For laypeople, the Buddha considered the righteous acquisition of wealth and financial security a skilful source of happiness. However, he warned against hoarding wealth, comparing it to digging one's own grave. Conversely, he likened the generous person to one with two eyes, while the stingy were compared to the one-eyed, highlighting the limited vision of those who fail to share.

In Buddhism, giving is considered a potent source of merit with lasting benefits, both in this life and in future rebirths. One manifestation of this is 'instant karma'—the immediate mental and emotional rewards of giving. The very act of generosity brings joy to the giver, as it arises from compassion and goodwill. The Buddha stressed that dana should be performed with delight before, during and after the act of giving. It is not meant to be obligatory or done begrudgingly but with a sincere and joyful heart.

At its core, dana means giving freely without expecting anything in return. It is motivated by compassion and the wish for another's well-being. However, in its highest form, giving is directed towards the cultivation of enlightenment. The Buddha taught that one should 'give gifts to adorn and beautify the mind', with adornments such as non-clinging, loving-kindness and genuine concern for others. Through generosity, practitioners cultivate a generous spirit, which is ultimately more significant than any single act of giving. After all, it is possible to give without being truly generous, but it is impossible to be genuinely generous without giving.

Though Buddhism is often associated with meditation, pacifism and simplicity, generosity is a central practice that is sometimes overlooked. The Buddha identified three core practices: dana (generosity), *sila* (ethical conduct) and *bhavana* (meditation). Together, these form the foundation of spiritual progress. Additionally, in both Theravada and Mahayana traditions, the cultivation of the *paramis* or *paramitas* is essential for attaining enlightenment. Generosity is the first of these perfections, highlighting its foundational importance.

The Practice of Generosity

In Buddhism, the intention behind giving is more important than the gift itself. The Buddha taught that offering even a small or seemingly insignificant gift, such as food scraps to insects, holds merit when given with a pure heart. However, giving valuable items to those in need is considered a greater act of generosity.

The Buddha described three ideal conditions for giving:

- **Pure gift:** Something appropriate and honestly earned.
- **Pure intentions:** Giving with compassion, free from selfish motives or harm.
- **Pure recipient:** A virtuous person or one genuinely in need.

While meeting these conditions is ideal, all acts of giving—no matter how small—are considered generous. In Buddhism, generosity extends beyond material charity. It includes everyday acts of kindness, such as helping a customer or offering a product with the sincere hope that it will benefit them. The thought behind the action is what truly matters.

Karmic Benefits of Generosity

The Buddha taught that giving brings both immediate and long-term benefits. In the present, it generates joy, reduces greed and cultivates goodwill. In the future, it generates positive karma, which can lead to favourable rebirths or material and spiritual blessings.

While material gain may seem uncharacteristically Buddhist, wealth is viewed as a potential means for further generosity. Historical benefactors such as Anathapindika, King Bimbisara and Emperor Ashoka played crucial roles in the growth of Buddhism through their patronage. The monastic community itself relies on the generosity of lay supporters for sustenance.

The Buddha, born a prince, relinquished his wealth in pursuit of enlightenment, but his ability to do so was made possible by his privileged position. Similarly, the resources and stability of those in modern society enable them to engage in spiritual practice and acts of generosity.

Spiritual Benefits of Generosity

Generosity in Buddhism is ultimately a spiritual practice. It trains the mind to let go of attachments and fosters altruism. By reducing greed and ill will—two of the primary obstacles to enlightenment—it supports spiritual progress. Though dana alone cannot lead to enlightenment, it is a powerful aid on the path. Generosity also transcends the boundaries of this life. According to Buddhist teachings, those who give with pure hearts generate karmic merit that leads to fortunate rebirths and spiritual advancement.

However, the Buddha considered the highest motivation for giving to be the pursuit of nibbana (nirvana). In this context, dana becomes more than an act of kindness—it is a step towards liberation.

Generosity for Others' Benefit

Generosity is not only a tool for personal growth but also a means of alleviating the suffering of others. Everyone, at some point, relies on the generosity of others, whether from parents, guardians or strangers. Acts of giving—whether building a hospital, providing a meal, or offering kindness—lighten the burdens of others. The ultimate embodiment of generosity is the Buddha himself. To become a Buddha requires perfecting oneself and selflessly giving over countless lifetimes. The Buddha's boundless generosity and tireless effort enabled him to attain enlightenment and share the *Dhamma* (dharma) with the world.

In Buddhism, the practice of generosity is linked to the cultivation of six far-reaching attitudes, known as the paramitas (perfections). These virtues are essential for personal development and the welfare of others. By counteracting obstacles like laziness, anger and ignorance, they guide practitioners towards spiritual awakening. The six paramitas are:

1. **Generosity (Dana)**: Freely offering material aid, protection, or kindness without expectation of return.
2. **Ethical self-discipline (Sila)**: Maintaining moral integrity and avoiding harmful actions.
3. **Patience (Kshanti)**: Bearing hardships and remaining calm in the face of adversity.
4. **Perseverance (Virya)**: Joyful effort and steadfastness in virtuous practices.

5. **Mental stability or concentration (Dhyana):**
   Developing focus and calmness of mind.
6. **Discriminating awareness or wisdom (Prajna):** Seeing
   reality clearly and acting with discernment.

These attitudes are considered far-reaching because, when
fully developed, they help transcend personal limitations
and overcome suffering. Practising them with renunciation
leads to liberation, while practising them with *bodhichitta*—
the aspiration to attain Buddhahood for the benefit of all
beings—leads to full enlightenment.

The Four Forms of Giving

In Buddhism, generosity takes multiple forms, each with
distinct benefits. The four primary forms of giving are:

Material Aid: This includes offering possessions, food,
clothing, money or other resources. It can also involve non-
material contributions, such as volunteering time or physical
effort. Even simple acts, like cleaning a shared space for
others' enjoyment, count as material aid.

Teachings and Advice: Sharing beneficial knowledge is
another form of generosity. In the Buddhist context, this
refers to sharing Dhamma teachings, but it extends to
everyday life. Offering guidance, tutoring a student, or giving
career advice are all acts of generous wisdom.

Protection from Fear: Alleviating the fear or distress of
others is also a form of giving. This includes rescuing animals
from harm, comforting frightened children, or offering
shelter to the vulnerable. Small acts, such as moving an
insect out of danger, also qualify.

Love: Generosity of love involves sincerely wishing for others'
happiness and well-being. It is not about physical affection

but about cultivating goodwill. A warm smile, kind words or compassionate thoughts can be powerful expressions of this form of generosity.

Generosity Beyond Wealth

In Buddhism, generosity is not restricted to material wealth. Even those with few possessions can cultivate a generous spirit. The Buddha encouraged practitioners to mentally share everything they enjoy—fresh air and beautiful sunsets. When possible, material giving and service naturally follow. Whether through time, effort or resources, giving joyfully and with a pure heart creates a powerful force of kindness. It benefits both the giver and the recipient, generating karma that leads to future happiness and prosperity.

By practising generosity, we follow the Buddha's example and contribute to a more compassionate and harmonious world.

CONFUCIANISM

In Confucianism, giving (*shi*) is not treated as an isolated virtue but is instead viewed within the broader framework of ren and yi, which are key concepts in Confucian thought.

Benevolence and Righteousness

Ren: Often translated as humaneness, compassion or perfect virtue, ren embodies kindness and concern for others. It is regarded as the highest expression of human nature. Mencius, a prominent Confucian philosopher, described ren as the compassion shown towards the widow, the orphan and the elderly. To give with ren is to offer from a place of sincere empathy and kindness.

Yi: Commonly translated as righteousness, yi denotes acting appropriately and morally, guided by a sense of justice rather than personal gain. Mencius described ren as the heart and yi as the path, illustrating that benevolent intention should lead to righteous actions. In the context of giving, yi ensures that the act is performed with integrity and respect.

In Confucianism, true generosity stems from a benevolent heart and manifests as righteous action. It extends beyond one's family to include the entire community. The saying, 'Attend to the elderly and young in your family and others as well,' reflects the expansive scope of Confucian generosity.

Reciprocity and Gratitude

Another key Confucian concept linked to giving is *shu* or reciprocity. The Silver Rule of Confucianism states: 'Do not do unto others what you would not want others to do unto you.'

This principle encourages individuals to consider the needs and dignity of others, promoting empathy in both giving and receiving. Giving in Confucianism is not transactional but relational—it nurtures harmonious relationships and expresses shared humanity.

Gratitude is equally emphasized. The saying, 'Remember what you received; forget what you gave,' reflects the ideal attitude towards generosity. It encourages recipients to be thankful, while reminding givers to let go of their deeds without seeking praise or reward.

The Ethics of Giving

In Confucianism, the manner of giving is as important as the act itself. Mencius illustrated this through his selective acceptance of gifts. He accepted smaller gifts given with sincerity but returned larger ones given with disrespect. This highlights the emphasis on intention and respect over material value. True generosity in Confucianism requires:

- **Respect:** Giving without making the recipient feel inferior or indebted.
- **Sincerity:** Offering with a pure heart and selfless motivation.
- **Humility:** Forgetting one's own generosity and avoiding self-congratulation.

Education as the Highest Form of Giving

Confucianism elevates education as the most profound form of giving. Confucius viewed the sharing of knowledge as a means of empowering individuals to become self-reliant and virtuous. By giving education, one fosters both personal and societal growth.

This aligns with the broader Confucian goal of cultivating a harmonious and morally upright society. Through teaching, mentoring and guiding others, individuals contribute to the betterment of the community.

Extending Giving to All Beings

Confucianism extends the concept of giving beyond human beings to include animals and the environment. This reflects a holistic sense of compassion. Caring for animals, preserving nature and showing respect for all living beings are considered acts of benevolence. This ecological dimension of Confucianism aligns with modern environmental ethics, promoting a sustainable and compassionate relationship with the natural world.

The Practice of Empathy in Giving

Empathy is fundamental to Confucian ethics. It is not viewed as a passive emotion but as an active engagement with the suffering and well-being of others. The Analects emphasize the importance of putting oneself in another's place to understand their needs and feelings.

Practical ways to cultivate empathy in Confucianism include:

Knowing Oneself: Self-awareness is the starting point for empathy. Confucius believed that understanding one's own emotions and values is crucial for understanding others. By reflecting on one's behaviour and motivations, individuals can better relate to and empathize with others.

Listening to Others: Active listening is vital for empathy. Confucius taught that listening with an open heart and mind helps individuals understand the perspectives and needs of others. This involves not only hearing words but also paying attention to non-verbal cues and emotions.

Knowing the Recipient: To be truly empathetic, one must know the other person well. This knowledge allows for a deeper connection and more meaningful support. Confucius advocated for taking the time to learn about others' backgrounds, experiences and feelings.

Mirroring Actions: Empathy can be demonstrated through mirroring the actions and behaviours of others. Confucius noted that by aligning one's actions with those of others, individuals show solidarity and understanding. This can include adopting similar body language or engaging in shared activities.

Fulfilling the Needs of Others: Empathy in Confucianism extends to meeting the practical and emotional needs of others. Confucius believed that true generosity involves understanding and addressing what others require to thrive.

Using Sensitive Language: Communication is a key aspect of empathy. Confucius emphasized the importance of choosing words carefully to show respect and understanding. Sensitive language can help build trust and foster positive relationships.

Practising Patience: Patience is a virtue closely linked to empathy. Confucius taught that being patient with others, especially in difficult situations, is a way of showing compassion and understanding. Patience allows individuals to fully appreciate and respond to the needs of others.

Showing Care and Concern: Demonstrating genuine care and concern for others is a hallmark of Confucian empathy. Confucius believed that empathetic leaders and individuals focus on finding solutions to problems and supporting others through their challenges.

In Confucianism, the Art of Giving is not merely an act of charity but an ethical expression of one's moral character. It reflects empathy, respect and a commitment to nurturing others. The goal is not only to alleviate suffering but also to foster social harmony and cultivate virtue.

5

Giving across the Globe

IN A WORLD OFTEN DOMINATED BY CHALLENGES AND negativity, acts of kindness hold the power to transform lives, nurture relationships and unite communities. Across different cultures, kindness is expressed through unique traditions that reflect deeply held values of compassion, hospitality and interconnectedness. By exploring these cultural practices, we can draw inspiration to integrate kindness into our daily lives, creating a ripple effect of positivity.

Greece

In ancient Greece, hospitality was more than a social custom—it was a sacred duty governed by Zeus Xenios, the god of foreigners and strangers. The concept of philoxenia (from *xenia*: stranger, and *philo*: care for) embodied this tradition of kindness towards travellers. Upon arriving at a household, a stranger was offered food and shelter before being questioned, regardless of their identity. In return, the guest was expected to show respect by being courteous and not overstaying their welcome. Violating these obligations was believed to invoke the wrath of Zeus Xenios.

This tradition is famously illustrated in Homer's epics. In *The Odyssey*, Odysseus frequently relies on the hospitality of strangers during his long journey home. Conversely, in *The Iliad*, the Greeks' outrage over Paris's abduction of Helen—breaking the host-guest code—demonstrates the severe consequences of dishonouring xenia.

Today, the spirit of philoxenia lives on in Greece through everyday acts of kindness. Locals often go out of their way to help tourists, offering directions, walking them to their destination or inviting them for a meal. This enduring practice reflects the cultural value of treating strangers with warmth and generosity.

Japan

Japan's culture of politeness is epitomized by the concept of *omotenashi*, which translates to the 'spirit of service'. Rooted in the centuries-old *sado* (tea ceremony), omotenashi involves anticipating and fulfilling guests' needs with meticulous care and sincerity, without expecting anything in return. During the tea ceremony, the host carefully prepares and presents the tea with perfect attention to detail, creating an atmosphere of harmony and respect.

This ethos of selfless hospitality extends to all aspects of Japanese life. In restaurants and shops, staff greet customers warmly with '*irasshaimase*' (welcome). *Shinkansen* (bullet train) cleaners bow to passengers and taxi drivers open doors for their customers. These small but consistent gestures reflect Japan's commitment to courtesy and service.

Another Japanese tradition of kindness is *senbetsu*, the practice of giving farewell gifts to someone embarking on a journey. Historically, this involved providing supplies to pilgrims, ensuring their comfort. Today, it has evolved into a thoughtful gesture of support and well-wishing, symbolizing the enduring importance of kindness in Japanese culture.

Italy

In Italy, the tradition of *caffè sospeso* (suspended coffee) embodies generosity and solidarity. Originating in Naples over a century ago, this practice involves buying an extra coffee for a stranger in need. When someone unable to afford a coffee visits the café, they can enjoy the pre-paid drink.

Beyond offering a warm beverage, caffè sospeso fosters a culture of community care. The gesture is anonymous and selfless, as the giver never meets the recipient. This practice has spread globally, inspiring similar initiatives in other countries, such as suspended meals and pay-it-forward schemes.

By participating in caffè sospeso, individuals contribute to a cycle of kindness, promoting empathy and compassion. This small act of generosity serves as a reminder that even the simplest gestures can brighten someone's day and strengthen social bonds.

South Africa

In South Africa, the philosophy of *ubuntu* expresses the interconnectedness of humanity. Derived from the Nguni languages, ubuntu is often encapsulated in the proverb, '*umuntu ngumuntu ngabantu*'—a person is a person through other persons. It conveys the belief that one's humanity is defined by their relationships with others.

During South Africa's transition from apartheid, ubuntu became a guiding principle of reconciliation. Nelson Mandela, a staunch advocate of ubuntu, described it as 'the profound sense that we are human only through the humanity of others.' His life's work exemplified this ethos, as he dedicated himself to promoting equality, forgiveness and compassion.

Desmond Tutu, another proponent of ubuntu, applied it during the Truth and Reconciliation Commission. His Christian perspective highlighted the values of forgiveness, generosity and peaceful coexistence. Tutu explained, 'You can't be human all by yourself. When you have ubuntu, you are known for your generosity.'

In practice, ubuntu encourages acts of kindness, compassion and solidarity. Whether helping a neighbour, sharing resources or offering emotional support, ubuntu promotes the idea that kindness strengthens the social fabric and enhances collective well-being.

Spain

Along the Camino de Santiago, a renowned pilgrimage route in Spain, locals demonstrate remarkable kindness and hospitality towards travellers. These benevolent individuals, often called the 'Angels of the Camino', offer invaluable support to pilgrims. They provide essential guidance to prevent travellers from losing their way and offer food and water to those in need. In many cases, these generous locals even open their homes or provide shelter to weary pilgrims, offering a safe haven where they can rest and rejuvenate.

This tradition of hospitality not only meets the pilgrims' physical needs but also offers emotional support, fostering a sense of community and belonging. The kindness shown by the 'Angels' embodies the true essence of generosity and community spirit. Their selfless acts create an atmosphere of warmth and compassion, greatly enriching the pilgrimage experience.

These small gestures—whether a simple smile, a helping hand or a warm meal—underscore the profound impact of generosity. By supporting the pilgrims in such meaningful ways, locals along the Camino de Santiago demonstrate how even the smallest acts of kindness can create a nurturing and supportive environment, making the arduous journey more bearable and spiritually fulfilling.

Myanmar

Despite facing significant poverty, Myanmar is renowned for its culture of generosity, deeply influenced by Theravada Buddhism. The practice of giving, or dana, is a cornerstone of Buddhist teachings and plays a vital role in daily life. It encourages individuals to donate food, clothing and money to support Buddhist monks and nuns, who rely entirely on these offerings for their sustenance. In turn, the monks often aid the less fortunate, creating a continuous cycle of giving and receiving that benefits the entire community.

This reciprocal relationship not only ensures the monks' basic needs are met but also extends compassion and assistance to the broader population, particularly those in dire need. Acts of kindness are not limited to religious settings; they permeate everyday life. It is common for community members to donate food to monasteries, which then distribute meals to the poorest residents. Clothing donations ensure the less fortunate receive essential items, while financial contributions support charitable initiatives, including healthcare and education programmes.

This pervasive spirit of giving fosters a strong sense of community, where individuals feel a collective responsibility to care for one another. It reflects the belief that by supporting each other, the entire society benefits, creating an environment where kindness and generosity are integral to social harmony and well-being.

Iran

Mashhad, nestled in the mountains of north-east Iran, usually sees its first snowfall in January. However, by December, the city already feels the chilling grip of winter. In December 2015, moved by concern for the city's substantial homeless population, an anonymous resident launched a creative initiative. He painted a wall with vibrant colours and installed pegs and hangers. Next to it, a message in Farsi read: 'If you don't need it, leave it. If you need it, take it.'

Kindness is deeply ingrained in Persian culture, and this gesture resonated with Mashhad's residents. They eagerly donated spare warm clothing. The concept quickly gained popularity on social media, and 'walls of kindness' began appearing throughout Iran and beyond, with each adaptation reflecting the original spirit of generosity.

This initiative beautifully exemplifies the culture of giving and community care in Persian society, where even simple acts of kindness can inspire widespread compassion and solidarity.

New Zealand

In New Zealand, the Maori principle of *kaitiakitanga*, meaning 'guardianship' or 'stewardship', highlights the cultural importance of caring for the environment. This principle reflects a deep respect and connection between people and nature, emphasizing that the health of the land, rivers and seas is directly linked to the well-being of the community.

One powerful example of kaitiakitanga is the recognition of the Whanganui River as a legal entity with rights equivalent to those of a person. This status, granted in 2017, acknowledges the river's significance and ensures that any harm to it is treated as harm to a human being. The Maori community fought for over a century to achieve this recognition, demonstrating their unwavering commitment to preserving the river for future generations.

Acts of kindness under kaitiakitanga extend beyond human interactions to include protecting and nurturing the environment. Local communities frequently organize clean-up events for beaches, rivers and forests, fostering a sense of collective responsibility and pride in maintaining these natural spaces. Sustainable resource management practices, such as regulated fishing and hunting, help ensure natural resources are used responsibly and remain abundant.

Education also plays a key role, with schools and community programmes teaching the importance of environmental stewardship. By promoting sustainable practices in agriculture and urban development, the Maori demonstrate that kindness can be extended not only to people but also to the natural world, creating a harmonious and sustainable environment for all.

China

In China, the principle of *mudita* revolves around taking genuine pleasure in the happiness and success of others. Rooted in Buddhist teachings, mudita encourages individuals to cultivate joy and mindfulness, transforming others' achievements into a source of personal happiness. This philosophy promotes acts of kindness and generosity, such as mentoring colleagues, celebrating friends' accomplishments and offering community support.

Through mudita, people learn to rejoice in others' success without envy, fostering a more harmonious and supportive social environment. Practical applications include guiding a colleague at work, actively participating in the celebrations of others' milestones and creating a positive atmosphere where everyone feels valued. By emphasizing the interconnectedness of individual well-being and community happiness, mudita helps build strong, resilient relationships that enrich the fabric of society.

Brazil

In Brazil, the concept of *gentileza gera gentileza*, or 'kindness begets kindness', is a powerful cultural belief that underscores the ripple effect of benevolent actions. This philosophy encourages people to inspire others through acts of kindness, fostering a more compassionate and supportive community.

The impact of this belief is evident in various community initiatives aimed at helping those in need and supporting local causes. Neighbours often assist each other with daily tasks, participate in clean-up projects and volunteer for social causes. These acts of kindness not only provide immediate help but also inspire others to continue the cycle of generosity.

The ethos of 'gentileza gera gentileza' promotes a culture in which kindness is contagious, and every act of generosity contributes to a more cohesive and caring society.

Scotland

In Scotland, the tradition of *ceilidh* gatherings plays a crucial role in fostering connection and community spirit. These social events, characterized by music, dance and storytelling, create a sense of belonging and mutual support. More than just entertainment, ceilidhs are a vital part of Scottish cultural life, strengthening bonds and promoting unity.

Acts of kindness at these gatherings often include sharing food, helping with event preparations and offering support to those in need. These interactions reinforce the value of unity and collective well-being. The spirit of the ceilidh extends beyond the events themselves, inspiring individuals to support each other in their daily lives.

Whether it is assisting a neighbour, providing emotional support or simply sharing a meal, these acts of kindness help build a resilient and tightly knit community. The ceilidh tradition highlights the importance of coming together, celebrating shared heritage and fostering an environment where everyone feels connected and valued.

The Philippines

In the Philippines, the spirit of *bayanihan* highlights unity and cooperation as neighbours come together to help one another, whether by building homes or offering support in times of hardship. Bayanihan exemplifies the power of kindness and the solidarity found in community care.

Acts such as volunteering for local projects, extending aid to those in need and promoting shared values are integral to this tradition. Bayanihan fosters a strong sense of belonging and demonstrates how collective compassion can uplift individuals and strengthen communities.

Denmark

In Denmark, the concept of *hygge* encompasses creating a warm, cosy and inviting atmosphere, often shared with others. Hygge encourages Danes to practise kindness through small, thoughtful gestures that enhance the comfort and well-being of those around them.

Examples of hygge include inviting friends over for a warm meal, sharing homemade treats or creating a welcoming space with candles and comfortable seating. This focus on shared moments of comfort and joy strengthens social bonds and promotes a culture of care and compassion.

Thailand

In Thailand, the practice of *nam jai*, which translates to 'water of the heart', represents acts of generosity and kindness that flow naturally and freely. Thais often demonstrate nam jai through actions such as offering food to neighbours, helping strangers or participating in community projects.

One prominent example is the tradition of giving alms to Buddhist monks, which not only supports the monks but also fosters a sense of spiritual connection and community involvement. This culture of giving is deeply embedded in Thai society, encouraging people to care for one another with genuine compassion.

Finland

In Finland, the concept of *talkoot* refers to community gatherings where people come together to perform voluntary work for the common good. Talkoot activities often involve building playgrounds, cleaning parks or assisting with agricultural tasks.

These events not only achieve practical goals but also strengthen community ties and foster a sense of solidarity. Finns believe that participating in talkoot is an important way to contribute to society and support one another, promoting a culture of mutual aid and cooperation.

Kenya

In Kenya, the practice of *harambee*, which means 'all pull together' in Swahili, represents collective community action. Harambee is often used to mobilize resources for communal projects, such as building schools, hospitals or wells. This tradition emphasizes the importance of working together for the common good and highlights the power of collective effort.

Acts of kindness inspired by harambee include organizing community fundraisers, volunteering for local projects and supporting neighbours in need. This strong sense of community cooperation is a cornerstone of Kenyan society, fostering solidarity and mutual care.

Bhutan

In Bhutan, the concept of 'gross national happiness' (GNH) reflects the country's commitment to prioritizing the well-being of its citizens over economic growth. This philosophy encourages acts of kindness and compassion as integral components of a happy and harmonious society.

Examples of kindness in Bhutan include community celebrations, collective agricultural work and support for environmental conservation efforts. The government's focus on GNH promotes policies that foster social support, environmental sustainability and cultural preservation, creating a society where kindness and well-being are central values.

Turkey

In Turkey, the tradition of *askıda ekmek*, or 'bread on the hook', is a simple yet profound act of kindness. This practice involves people buying an extra loaf of bread at a bakery and leaving it 'on the hook' for someone in need to take.

This gesture ensures that those who cannot afford bread have access to food. The askıda ekmek tradition reflects Turkish values of generosity and community support, encouraging people to look out for one another and provide for the less fortunate.

Iceland

In Iceland, the concept of *þjóðaratkvæðagreiðsla*, or 'national referendum', embodies the country's commitment to collective decision-making and shared responsibility. While this term typically applies to politics, the underlying principle of community involvement extends to everyday acts of kindness.

Icelanders frequently participate in communal activities such as neighbourhood clean-ups, maintaining public spaces and supporting local initiatives. These acts of kindness strengthen social bonds and foster a culture of cooperation and mutual respect.

Russia

In Russia, the tradition of *pomochi* involves neighbours and community members coming together to help one another with tasks requiring collective effort. This can include building homes, harvesting crops or repairing communal infrastructure.

Pomochi reflects the value Russians place on mutual assistance and solidarity, particularly in rural areas where community support is essential. Acts of kindness inspired by pomochi include providing food and shelter to those in need, sharing resources and offering help during emergencies.

United States

In the US, the concept of 'paying it forward' encourages acts of kindness and community support. This practice involves performing a good deed for someone without expecting anything in return, with the hope that the recipient will continue the chain of kindness.

Examples include paying for the next person's coffee, leaving money in a vending machine for the next user or helping someone carry their groceries. These actions create a ripple effect of compassion and generosity.

Additionally, community volunteering is widespread in the US, with people dedicating their time to soup kitchens, shelters and local non-profits. These efforts reinforce a strong culture of giving and mutual support.

Canada

In Canada, the tradition of 'neighbourly acts' is deeply ingrained in the culture, emphasizing the importance of helping one another in times of need. For instance, during harsh winters, Canadians often shovel snow for elderly neighbours or assist with other tasks made challenging by extreme weather.

Another common act of kindness is the 'Toonie Drive', where people donate two-dollar coins to support charitable causes, showing how small contributions can make a significant impact. These acts foster a strong sense of community and solidarity, ensuring that everyone feels supported and cared for.

Australia

In Australia, the tradition of 'mateship' plays a crucial role in fostering community spirit and mutual support. Mateship embodies values of loyalty, equality and friendship, encouraging Australians to look out for one another.

Acts of kindness inspired by mateship include helping neighbours during natural disasters, such as bushfires and floods, organizing community fundraisers and offering support to friends and strangers alike.

Initiatives like 'Clean Up Australia Day' further demonstrate this spirit, as volunteers work together to clean local environments, highlighting their commitment to preserving and protecting their country for future generations.

Norway

In Norway, the concept of *dugnad* refers to voluntary community work where people collaborate to achieve a shared goal. Dugnad activities often involve maintaining local parks, cleaning communal areas or organizing neighbourhood events.

This tradition fosters a sense of community and shared responsibility, ensuring that everyone contributes to the well-being of their surroundings. Additionally, Norwegians often perform acts of kindness during winter, such as checking on elderly neighbours and helping with snow removal. These practices highlight the importance of community solidarity and mutual support in Norwegian society.

South Korea

In South Korea, the concept of *jeong* refers to a deep feeling of affection and bonding that develops over time. Acts of kindness inspired by jeong include sharing food with neighbours, helping friends and family in need and caring for the elderly.

One common practice is the preparation and sharing of kimchi, a traditional Korean dish, among neighbours and friends. This act of sharing not only provides sustenance but also strengthens community ties.

Additionally, South Koreans often engage in volunteer work, supporting local charities and organizations to help the less fortunate, fostering a culture of compassion and solidarity.

◆

These global examples show that kindness knows no boundaries of culture or geography. By embracing and practising acts of kindness, we can help build a compassionate and connected world community. Let these stories inspire us to perform our own acts of kindness—whether small gestures or larger efforts—as each action has the power to bring about positive change and foster a more compassionate world.

Positivity is the best way to sustainable success.

SECTION II

The Philosophy in Action

6

Art of Giving over the Years

AS I REFLECT ON THE JOURNEY THAT LED TO THE CREATION and evolution of the Art of Giving, I am reminded of its humble beginnings and the profound impact it has had over the years. My own life story, marked by early adversity and a resolve to aid others, has been the bedrock of this initiative.

Born into poverty and faced with the tragic loss of my father at a young age, I experienced first-hand the struggles and the urgent need for compassion in our society. From performing small acts of giving as a child to establishing a global movement, the concept of giving has been deeply ingrained in my actions and philosophy.

The Art of Giving was born out of a deep desire to formalize the instinct of generosity that has driven me throughout my life. This initiative was not just about charity, but about fostering a culture of kindness, compassion and mutual respect across all boundaries. It is a philosophy of life that aspires to promote happiness and peace by transcending borders, castes, creeds and nationalities, strengthened by the bonds of humanity.

Over the years, the Art of Giving has grown from a personal commitment into a worldwide movement. With each passing year, we have introduced new themes and activities that resonate with the pressing issues of the times, encouraging widespread participation.

The growth of the Art of Giving movement has been exponential, transforming it into a volunteer-driven campaign that encourages people to practise the Art of Giving in their daily lives. It has become a platform that connects those in need with those who have the means to give, fostering a global community of givers. This initiative has proven that when we give, we do not merely help others—we create a state of happiness within ourselves and promote a healthier society.

For the last nine years, the Art of Giving community, consisting of well-wishers and those inspired by it, has celebrated 17 May as the International Day of the Art of Giving. Each year, we embrace a unique theme reflecting the spirit of kindness, compassion and service:

- **2015 – Kompassion: The Garment Bank:** People donated old clothes to the needy, promoting sustainable giving.
- **2017 – Cyclothon:** An event promoting environmental awareness, fitness and self-care through cycling.
- **2018 – Pyaar Bhara Pack:** Over 20 million meals were distributed, bringing nourishment and comfort to countless individuals.
- **2019 – Bag of Happiness:** People united by gifting happiness kits to students, filled with essential school supplies and treats.
- **2020 – AOG Fights Corona:** In response to the pandemic, this theme acknowledged COVID warriors and provided aid to victims, embodying resilience and solidarity.
- **2021 – My Mother, My Hero:** The AOG community expressed gratitude by writing heartfelt letters to mothers, the ultimate givers.
- **2022 – Hope, Happiness and Harmony:** The focus was on supporting one another through simple acts of love, compassion, empathy, kindness and gratitude.

- **2023 – Helping the Help:** Celebrating a decade of the Art of Giving, we honoured and supported those who help us in daily life—teachers, postmen, drivers, janitors and many more.
- **2024 – Let's AOG:** The theme aimed to transform the Art of Giving from a specific action into a way of life, open to personal interpretation and application by everyone.

Since 2017, the Art of Giving family has grown from thousands to millions with the introduction of community contribution for community building. The movement has evolved into what it was always meant to be: by the public, of the public and for the public.

With over 1.5 million active members and conveners in over 300 locations worldwide, the Art of Giving has touched approximately 10 million lives through both direct actions and social media interactions. This engagement highlights the power of digital platforms in spreading our message and rallying support across diverse populations.

Reflecting on this decade-long journey, it is clear that what began as a small seed has blossomed into a global festival of kindness. Our initiatives have covered a broad spectrum—from disaster relief to sustainable rural development—demonstrating the wide-reaching capabilities of this movement.

As I continue to live by this philosophy, my hope is that it will inspire others to do the same, creating a ripple effect that transforms the world into a more harmonious and compassionate place. It is a reminder that through simple acts of giving, we can confront the challenges of today and build a brighter future for all.

7

KIIT and KISS as Examples of the Art of Giving

MY STORY OF STRUGGLE, POVERTY, HUNGER AND humiliation is not unknown. I never thought I would ever make it big in life. I somehow managed to get a basic education and, against all odds, started a lectureship at the age of 22. By the time I was 25, I had founded KIIT and KISS in a modest two-room rented apartment. From these humble beginnings, God propelled it to the level it is today—both institutions have attained global recognition and national acclaim.

In 1992–93, India was opening its doors to liberalization, privatization and globalization. The License-Permit-Quota Raj was gradually giving way to economic reforms, creating new opportunities. Yet, Odisha was still struggling. The state was only known for its issues of natural calamities, poverty, hunger and malnutrition, rather than for development or progress.

Poverty creates illiteracy.
Literacy eradicates poverty.

At the time, private education in Odisha was largely limited to schools. Higher education lacked strong private institutions, not only in the state but across much of the country. Odisha was grappling with the irony of being rich in resources yet poor in reality.

I had no family pedigree or inheritance to fall back on. The banking system was not as open as it is today, and loans were difficult to secure. In the early years of building KIIT and KISS, I took small loans of ₹10,000–₹20,000 from friends and acquaintances.

For every new pillar or addition to the institution, I would sit and ponder over whom to approach for funds. I made sure not to ask the same people repeatedly, striving to give them confidence that I would repay their loans. While many refused outright, some believed in me and extended their support.

By the end of 1995, my outstanding hand loans had reached ₹16 lakh. Creditors began asking for their money, but I had no means to repay them. The financial stress was overwhelming, and I found myself hiding from those I owed, ashamed and helpless.

There came a time when I felt utterly defeated. Believing that I would never be able to repay my debts, I considered ending my life. I thought that suicide was the only way to escape the trap I was in. But something stopped me—perhaps it was divine intervention or a higher purpose. That fateful night became the turning point of my life.

With God's grace and relentless persistence, Punjab National Bank sanctioned a ₹25 lakh term loan. I repaid ₹10 lakh to my creditors and used the remaining amount to begin construction of Campus 1, which is now known as Koel Campus. From that point onwards, there was no looking back. KIIT and KISS steadily grew, transforming into institutions of excellence and social impact. What started as a dream built on borrowed funds became a beacon of hope and empowerment.

◆

If I go down memory lane, north Bhubaneswar in 1992–93 was nothing like it is today. From NALCO Square to Nandankanan, an 8 km stretch, the area was largely barren. Apart from Patia village, the region was sparsely populated, with a few Housing Board colony houses scattered around. People associated the area with snake charmers and feared venturing there after dusk.

Against all odds, I chose to build KIIT and KISS in this isolated area. Today, the campus spans 36 sq. km and has transformed the entire north Bhubaneswar region. The area now boasts the highest density of businesses and residents, and is a major educational and commercial hub. With the upcoming metro line, KIIT will become one of the most important junctions in the city, symbolizing the area's transformation from wilderness to a thriving metropolis.

Before 2005, students from Odisha would board special trains to Hyderabad and Bangalore to sit for entrance exams in South Indian colleges. Thousands of aspiring teens sought quality higher education outside the state. However, KIIT changed this dynamic. Today, students from South India and over 70 other countries come to Bhubaneswar to study at KIIT and KISS.

The once overlooked city is now a global educational hub, attracting talent and fostering academic excellence. Our efforts have turned Bhubaneswar into a cosmopolitan city, making it an educational destination. Today, about 95 per cent of KIIT's students come from outside Odisha, and thousands of people visit the campus every year.

While industries are often celebrated for their large-scale impact, academic institutions rarely receive the same recognition—despite their significant contributions to society. KIIT and KISS have set a remarkable example of how education can be a powerful agent of change. From the beginning, these institutions have championed kindness, compassion and humanitarianism, creating a culture of inclusivity.

KIIT and KISS have not only transformed north Bhubaneswar but have also uplifted marginalized communities through free education, healthcare and livelihood support. Following the ideals of the Radhakrishnan Commission, KIIT espouses sympathy for the poor, respect for women, and the promotion of love and peace, while KISS has empowered thousands of tribal children, offering them a future filled with hope and opportunity.

By promoting KIIT, KISS and Odisha across India and abroad, I have, by the blessings of the Almighty, become somewhat of a brand ambassador for Odisha.

◆

When people hear about my poverty-stricken childhood and unremarkable education, they often find it difficult to believe what I have achieved. But I always say God has done it. I am merely the medium, and I am grateful to be that medium.

I had never visited or imagined I would build an institution akin to the likes of Harvard, Oxford, Cambridge or Stanford. Yet, in just 25 years, KIIT and KISS have built an ecosystem comparable to university cities that took centuries to evolve.

From a two-room apartment to a globally recognized institution, this journey is a testament to the power of resilience, faith and service. It is a reminder that adversity can be the foundation for greatness when paired with unwavering determination and a spirit of giving.

◆

Many education leaders tell me that while people make educational institutions, few have been able to make them as popular, visible and beautiful as we have. From a rented two-room training centre to a huge, world-class campus is indeed a marvel that everyone cherishes today.

Right from the start, I had a clear vision of the kind of facilities I wanted for KIIT. When I began constructing what is today known as Campus 3, the founding campus for engineering, I envisioned a beautiful campus with lawns and greenery.

At the time, some people ridiculed me. They questioned whether I was building a hotel rather than an educational institution. However, I was certain that the requirement of the present age was not just academic excellence but also a serene and inspiring environment. Today, even those who once mocked me acknowledge that it was the right decision. From that modest beginning, KIIT now has 30 campuses, and I feel blessed by God's grace for the appreciation and praise that continues to pour in from all corners of the world.

◆

We began hosting seminars, summits, meets, congresses and conferences as early as 1997, which I consider the base year of KIIT and KISS. These events provided immense exposure to Bhubaneswar, making it a centre of academic and intellectual exchange.

In 2001, we hosted the biggest conference of the time—the Indian Society of Technical Education conference—which welcomed around 2,000 academicians and policymakers. This event marked a significant milestone, bringing Bhubaneswar into the limelight.

Subsequently, we hosted a series of prestigious events, including:

- The Indian Science Congress
- The Indian Economic Association Conference, graced by the then Prime Minister Manmohan Singh

- The World Anthropology Congress
- The World Congress of Poets
- The South Asian Women's Conference
- The Commonwealth Big Lunch

So far, around 22 Nobel laureates have visited our campus and delivered lectures. These events have not only enhanced KIIT's reputation but have also contributed to building Brand Odisha—showcasing the state as a centre of academic and cultural excellence on the global stage.

We have also made significant strides in sports since 2000.

- In 2009, we constructed the first indoor stadium, a landmark facility that enhanced the sporting culture of the region.
- Today, around 1,50,000 participants come to KIIT and KISS annually to engage in sports and other extracurricular activities.
- For nearly 15 years, we have hosted the Grandmaster Chess tournament, attracting participants from 30 countries, further cementing our global reach.

KIIT has led the way in securing academic affiliations and global rankings, setting benchmarks for other institutions to follow. We were among the first universities to:

- Achieve internationalization of education
- Build brand trust among parents, students and stakeholders through quality and consistency
- Gain national and international recognition that reaffirm our credibility

What is now common for most universities was started by KIIT, making us a trailblazer in branding and quality assurance in higher education. In 2019, KIIT earned the prestigious 'Institution of Eminence' status—a recognition that affirms its place among India's top universities.

Today, KIIT is a conglomerate of institutions offering education and training across diverse disciplines, including engineering, medical and dental studies, jurisprudence, management, nursing, biotechnology, film and media, humanities and many other subjects.

Kalinga Institute of Social Sciences

Not only is Odisha poor and affected by natural calamities every other year but the state is also home to a large tribal population, constituting one-fourth of its people. Many of them live in remote forests without basic amenities and are largely unaware of education, healthcare and other essential public services. A majority endure abject poverty, hunger, malnutrition and illiteracy.

In 1992–93, KIIT established the Kalinga Institute of Social Sciences, exclusively for the poorest tribal children. KISS has since grown into the largest residential tribal institution in the world, serving 80,000 tribal students (30,000 in KISS Bhubaneswar, 40,000 alumni and 10,000 in satellite centres across 10 districts of Odisha). At KISS, children receive free education, food, accommodation and healthcare from KG to PhD. In 2017, it was accorded 'University' status by the Ministry of Human Resource Development, Government of India, becoming the world's first fully residential, free tribal university.

KISS, which began with just 125 underprivileged tribal students, is indeed a great gift to the community. The institute collaborates with the United Nations and international agencies like the United Nations Development Programme (UNDP), the United Nations International Children's Emergency Fund (UNICEF) and United Nations Volunteers on capacity building in tribal education. It operates with the support of various stakeholders and well-wishers of KIIT, following an innovative financial model developed by me.

Periphery Development

Though KIIT's contribution to society cannot be quantified, its impact spans every aspect of life. With KIIT established on the outskirts of the city, the area has witnessed tremendous commercial and social growth.

Land prices have surged from ₹30,000 per acre in 1993 to ₹20 crore today. Shopping complexes, residential houses, hotels and restaurants now dot the area, employing thousands and generating substantial revenue for the state.

Idle youth, once vulnerable to crime, are now responsible, employed citizens contributing to the area's growth. KIIT directly employs 500 local youth in various capacities. Additionally, several educational institutions have emerged in the vicinity. KIIT has created direct employment for over 10,000 people and indirect employment for 2,00,000, driving business expansion and significantly reducing the crime rate. The once-deserted outskirts have transformed into a 'city within the city' of Bhubaneswar.

Skill Development and Entrepreneurship

Skill development and entrepreneurship promotion are integral to KIIT's mission. Since 1992, through its own training programmes and initiatives such as the Deen Dayal Upadhyaya Grameen Kaushalya Yojana (DDU-GKY), KIIT has trained over 50,000 skilled individuals. These students earn ITI (Industrial Training Institute) and polytechnic certificates in various trades.

Further, KIIT trains 5,000 youth annually, enabling

them to secure employment across the country under DDU-GKY and other Government of India and Government of Odisha schemes. An exemplary 'Job Mela' was held in Kandhamal parliamentary constituency in January 2020, where 80 companies offered 7,000 jobs to rural, unemployed youth with Class 10 education.

Creating Entrepreneurs

KIIT has groomed 100 successful entrepreneurs. Additionally, 100 more have emerged from KIIT-TBI (Technology Business Incubator).

Internationalization

A decade ago, KIIT had little visibility beyond Odisha, further hindered by the absence of an international airport in Bhubaneswar. However, KIIT has since made significant strides in internationalizing higher education. It has signed over 350 MoUs (memoranda of understanding) in India and abroad and holds memberships in all major international educational agencies.

KIIT has earned the prestigious Internationalization Strategies Advisory Service (ISAS) Badge from the International Association of Universities (IAU). Today, 2,000 foreign students from 65 countries are enrolled, while over 2,000 alumni have already graduated. In addition to short-term courses for foreign students, KIIT hosts hundreds of international and national seminars, workshops and conferences throughout the year.

Sports

Recognizing that academics and sports complement each other, KIIT has prioritized world-class sports infrastructure.

It offers facilities for 32 sports, including an international-standard swimming pool, archery ground, rugby ground, football field, hockey ground and a BCCI-approved cricket stadium, among others.

In 2020, KIIT successfully hosted the first-ever Khelo India University Games (KIUG) on its campus, followed by the Silver Jubilee Celebration of the All India Forest Sports Meet (AIFGM).

KIIT and KISS have produced 5,000 athletes competing at international, national, state and university levels. KIIT is the only university in India to have produced Olympians and gold medallists at the World University Games, while its students have also represented India in the Asiad, Commonwealth and other international sporting events.

No other Indian university matches KIIT's infrastructure and commitment to nurturing sportspersons.

Tourism

Since its inception (1997 is the base year), KIIT has been organizing hundreds of national and international seminars, workshops and conferences, inviting thousands of luminaries from India and abroad to Bhubaneswar. These contribute significantly to tourism in the state. It is common for people in the travel and tourism industry to say that 20 per cent of seats on every flight into and out of Bhubaneswar are reserved for KIIT stakeholders and students. The institute also has tremendous contributions in the fields of art, literature, culture, tourism, spiritualism and many others.

Rural Development

KIIT has made significant contributions to rural development since its establishment. In 2000, just three years after its founding, KIIT began transforming the remote village of Kalarabanka in the Cuttack district, approximately 60 km from Bhubaneswar, into a model and eventually a smart village. Once lacking essential facilities, Kalarabanka is now recognized as the only smart village in the country, and the entire panchayat has been developed into a model panchayat. City-like amenities have been introduced, including a residential high school, a nationalized bank with lockers and an ATM, a police station, a post office, Kalinga English Medium School, the Kalinga Institute of Medical Sciences (KIMS) Rural Health Centre with telemedicine facilities, a public library, a public park, a children's park, a drinking water project, concrete roads, streetlights and a Citizen's Knowledge & Service Centre among others.

Healthcare

As the saying goes, 'health is wealth'; therefore, healthcare is essential for every society and its people. KIIT boasts a large medical college, dental college and a 2,600-bed multi-specialty hospital, making significant contributions to Odisha's healthcare sector.

The University Medical College and Hospital and the Dental College and Hospital serve as medical hubs for local and regional communities. The 2,600-bed super-speciality hospital offers round-the-clock critical care services and provides free OPD (Outpatient Department) treatment to 2,000 patients daily.

KIIT organizes health camps in 20 blocks of the backward districts of Kandhamal, Boudh, Nayagarh and Ganjam on the third Sunday of every month. Additionally, it conducts healthcare awareness programmes to sensitize people on education, healthcare, malnutrition, hunger, poverty and environmental protection.

KIIT and KIMS plan to make Odisha disease-free by establishing 100 rural hospitals, each with a 100-bed capacity.

COVID-19

During the COVID-19 pandemic, KIIT swiftly opened a 500-bed COVID-19 hospital on the KIMS campus. This facility included a 50-bed ICU (Intensive Care Unit) and a 500-bed back-up hospital.

Additionally, KIIT set up three more 200-bed COVID-19 hospitals with necessary manpower in Kandhamal, Bolangir and Mayurbhanj districts, catering to the healthcare needs of these regions.

Helping One and All

KIIT has a proven track record of supporting people in distress, both in Odisha and beyond. The beneficiaries include poor women, girls and boys.

During the COVID-19 crisis, KIIT worked relentlessly from day one of the lockdown. In addition to opening and operating the hospitals, KIIT also:

- Distributed food packets to nearly 40,000 needy families in and around Bhubaneswar once a week (every Sunday) to ensure adequate nutrition and protein intake for slum children. This initiative continued for 21 days after the lockdown.
- Provided working lunch packets to around 1,200 police personnel stationed in Bhubaneswar for seven days, with due permission from the relevant department.
- Offered cooked food to stray animals (dogs and cows) across Bhubaneswar, and supplied green vegetables

to thousands of monkeys at various locations in the city.

- Provided skills training to 15,000 rural youth from Kandhamal and its neighbouring districts.

Community Development

The KIIT Community Engagement Cell (CEC) has launched an innovative initiative to develop 12 panchayats from 12 blocks of Kandhamal—an aspirational district with a 75 per cent Scheduled Caste and Scheduled Tribe population—into more liveable and prosperous communities. KIIT continues to work tirelessly to enhance employability and improve living standards in the region.

A University with a Difference

KIIT is truly a university with a difference—a private university in public service that embodies the spirit of humanitarian compassion. Since its inception, it has been deeply committed to constructive community engagement.

I firmly believe that universities solely focused on teaching and issuing certificates—without contributing to social progress—have little value and serve no meaningful purpose. I am heartened that my enthusiasm for serving society has inspired the entire KIIT staff, who now share this vision. I am confident that KIIT will continue expanding its community development efforts and grow from strength to strength.

KIIT seeks the good wishes and blessings of all to succeed in its noble mission.

8

Leading by Example

Festivity and Friends

INDIA IS A LAND OF FESTIVALS AND FESTIVITIES, WHERE countless celebrations, both big and small, unite its diverse population. The rituals, rites, traditions and legacy associated with each festival make the country vibrant and culturally rich.

Eastern India celebrates many festivals with great zeal and vigour. West Bengal and Odisha, in particular, celebrate Durga Puja with immense devotion and fervour. As the Puja approaches, an air of festivity envelops the region and its people. Schools and colleges close for the Puja break, and the advent of autumn, marked by the sight of kaash flowers, stirs memories and excitement for the fun and blessings that Maa Durga brings. People go on shopping sprees, buy new products, and plan trips with family and friends.

My Durga Puja itinerary is distinct and fixed. Despite my hectic schedule, I make it a point to visit my native village. There is an indescribable joy in reconnecting with one's roots. I cherish meeting school and village friends, reminiscing about old times and sharing moments of happiness with them. I have maintained this tradition for 30 years.

I reconnect with everyone in the village, especially my school batchmates, numbering over a hundred. Most alumni of the school, located in a remote village of Odisha, are not well-placed. By God's grace, I have supported about

80 of my 100 friends over the last three decades. Around 40 of them, or their children, are now employed at KIIT and KISS, leading fulfilled lives. Another 40 friends receive monthly financial aid, which I fondly call 'Friend Pension'. The joy this brings me is immeasurable.

The bond of friendship, love and compassion between my school friends and me remains as strong as ever. They reciprocate my love in full measure—this is my greatest treasure. Because I remain a simple and humble person, my interactions with them have not changed at all. I talk to them about their joys and sorrows. Their happiness becomes my own, and their challenges become mine.

On the immersion day of Maa Durga, a day after Dussehra, we all gather for dinner—an event I look forward to every year. I give Puja bakshish to thousands in the KIIT, KISS and KIMS ecosystems and beyond. Having never received chocolates or sweets during festive periods as a child, I understand the pain of deprivation.

All I wish for during the Puja festivities is to spread happiness and bring smiles to people's faces.

Lifelong Gratitude

I attended the 11th-day ritual of the Late Manorama Mohapatra of Keonjhar in 2021 and prayed for her departed soul to rest in peace. At her mourning ceremony, I fondly remembered our strong bond and the significant role she played in my life.

Back in 1994, during KIIT's formative stage, we were struggling financially and had finalized a plot on Nandankanan Road to set up the campus. We wanted to buy the land as it met all our requirements, but tracing the owners was difficult. In those days, without the internet, finding landowners in the less-developed areas of Bhubaneswar was a challenge. We eventually discovered that the owners were a mother-son duo from Keonjhar. But that did not solve the problem. We still did not know how to pay for the plot.

I travelled to Keonjhar, an eight-hour journey back then, and took a leap of faith by requesting the owners to let me pay in instalments. I knew I was asking for too much. I proposed paying 50 per cent of the agreed amount upfront, with the rest deferred until I could gather the funds. To my surprise, the owners agreed.

They allowed me to establish the campus on their land by paying only half the price upfront. This was the first piece of land ever bought for KIIT—the world now knows it as Campus 1.

Had they not agreed and trusted a struggling stranger, KIIT would not be what it is today. It marked the beginning of KIIT's growth—the rest is history.

The landowner, Manorama Mohapatra, treated me like her son. She was a pious soul, deeply involved in social work. Her son, inspired by our mission, later started a school for 300 orphans, empowering them holistically. We continue to support their cause from time to time.

At the mourning ceremony, I said, 'Be true to the salt you eat.'

Gratitude is my way of life. If anyone has ever helped me, I try to give back as much as I can, for as long as I can, and remain indebted for life.

After all, gratitude is the truest form of compassion.

Service before Self

Happiness is found in serving others and dedicating oneself to the service of humanity. It multiplies when an individual's actions become an inspiration for others to follow. Happiness grows exponentially when people embrace one's philosophy to achieve the greatest good in their own capacity. In this way, the value of inspiration increases, providing greater impetus for selfless service.

I want to introduce my readers to Ganesh G. Mundhe, a junior executive at Siemens Limited in Aurangabad, and Nikesh Bhogilal Madare, a contractual teacher at Shri M.S. Jain Special School in Jalna, Maharashtra.

These two gentlemen, both great well-wishers and ardent followers of the Art of Giving, were deeply inspired after watching the KISS Mega Kitchen episode on National Geographic a few years ago. They searched for my contact details for nearly two years before finally visiting KIIT and KISS, much to my pleasant surprise. Their only wish was to see KIIT and KISS and meet me once.

Destiny favours the determined—we finally met two years before the pandemic. Since then, they have been practising the philosophy of the Art of Giving in letter and spirit, thought and action.

They founded the Divya Jyoti Foundation and are uplifting the differently abled. They are inspired by our resilience and success, while I am moved by their commitment to give back to society, despite their modest lives and financial struggles.

True giving is not bound by wealth—it is driven by pure intentions. And that is how they transform their own lives by making a difference in society.

Nikesh, despite being visually impaired, refuses to let tragedy dissuade him from academic pursuits. He has completed his PhD and is one of the first visually impaired individuals to submit a doctoral thesis in his field. Despite challenging circumstances that make it difficult to sustain charitable activities, Nikesh has continued his selfless work with his friend.

Their social service is an example for others to follow. They have been visiting me annually since their first visit to KIIT and KISS. We often discuss our work and initiatives to make the world a better place.

I firmly believe that with strong willpower and the right intentions, one can achieve their dreams—and even more.

Such strong-hearted individuals, with a robust will to serve society unconditionally, make this world more liveable by alleviating suffering, one step at a time.

What You Sow, You Reap

I simply pen down my experiences. I am neither a prolific writer nor an acclaimed author. As someone always immersed in work, I rarely have time to read books or newspapers. I write from the heart—my experiences are my content, and my simplicity is my lucidity. What I am about to share may seem like a simple incident, but it carries a profound meaning and message.

Most people know that I live alone in a rented apartment—a humble residence that reflects my ethos of simple living. I have earned this lifestyle through adversity, turning it into an advantage as a self-made man. I enjoy doing my own work as much as feasible.

While I am an enthusiastic cook, my busy schedule often prevents me from indulging in this hobby. When a staff member who helped me at home tested positive for COVID-19, he took 75 days to recover. During this time, I had to handle the household chores myself, including making tea, which I thoroughly enjoyed.

In his absence, I began making tea not just for myself but also for the security guards on the morning and night shifts. I would serve them tea along with three to four types of savouries and biscuits.

I noticed their happiness, sometimes shy smiles, and quiet pride in being treated like family. This simple gesture became a regular morning and evening ritual, bringing immense joy to both them and me.

I have continued this practice to this day. These security guards have been with us for the last 10–15 years. They have always been content with their job of guarding the house. Although we had occasional chats, I had never spent much time with them before. The pandemic and the absence of my staff gave me the opportunity to connect with them and share moments of unspoken emotions.

To my surprise, the guards began doing extra chores around the house without being asked or seeking recognition. They would quietly clean the house, wash the dishes, water the plants and perhaps do much more that went unnoticed. The morning house help was astonished to find all the chores completed with no pending tasks. After years of routine, they suddenly took on extra duties, quietly expressing their gratitude in the humblest of ways.

When we show kindness to those who are less advantaged, they often reciprocate in unexpected ways. We need to spread kindness, and it will return to us in beautiful forms.

We must have patience. It is not always easy to show kindness to the less privileged, but it is a skill worth cultivating.

My humble beginnings taught me the value of kindness, and I urge my readers, friends and well-wishers to cultivate it as well. It might be painstaking, but it costs nothing. It is the best investment, as it brings reciprocation. And even if it does not, as the *Bhagavad Gita* exhorts, it still leaves one deeply happy.

Given the opportunity, the weak, too, can excel.

9

Real-Life Examples of Art of Giving from KISS

KISS STANDS AS AN OASIS OF HOPE, TRANSFORMATION and revolution for marginalized communities, particularly tribal children in Odisha and beyond.

It has grown into the world's largest free residential educational institution for indigenous children, offering holistic education from kindergarten to the postgraduate level. The institute ensures not only academic growth but also the overall development of its students.

KISS has empowered thousands of tribal children, equipping them with the skills and confidence to break the cycle of poverty and contribute meaningfully to society. It offers a unique blend of academic rigour, life-skills training and exposure to cultural diversity within a nurturing environment.

Giving quality education to a deprived child is like giving sight to the blind.

The institution has been instrumental in transforming the lives of countless students, providing them with opportunities that would have otherwise been beyond their reach. By fostering an inclusive and supportive community, KISS helps students realize their full potential and emerge as confident, self-reliant individuals, ready to make a positive impact in their communities and beyond. I would now like to narrate a few shining examples of this transformational impact.

Hara Prasad Hepruka, Sarpanch of Kuli Gram Panchayat, Rayagada

Born on 10 February 1992 to Kandha parents in the remote village of Utkapadu, Rayagada, Hara Prasad Hepruka faced significant challenges growing up. Despite his family's financial struggles, his parents recognized the value of education and worked hard to provide opportunities for their children.

Hara completed his schooling and then enrolled at KISS (Deemed University), where he earned a Master's degree in Political Science in 2013. Today, he serves as the sarpanch of Kuli gram panchayat in Rayagada, exemplifying the transformative power of KISS. His tenure has been marked by significant achievements, including COVID-19 awareness efforts recognized by the Chief Minister's Office, and his panchayat received the 'Sushta Panchayat Award' for excellence.

Growing up in a remote village with limited educational facilities, Hara initially lacked ambition and direction. His interactions with school teachers inspired him to pursue teaching. Though higher education seemed unattainable due to financial constraints, learning about KISS offered him the chance to pursue his studies without burdens.

Hara believes KISS helps the marginalized become productive and socially useful. It provided him with a renewed life and extensive educational exposure, allowing him to lead a dignified existence and integrate into mainstream society. He views his position in civil society as a significant achievement, made possible by KISS.

Before joining KISS, Hara was unaware of the institution, but once there, he found a supportive environment with clean classrooms and exceptional academic resources, including a 24/7 library, computer labs, free coaching, and access to books and newspapers.

As someone from a less-developed area, he found guidance at KISS to identify his skills and talents. The institution offered life-skills education, cultural activities and co-curricular events, enhancing his development. Influential guest lecturers broadened his horizons and deepened his understanding of the academic world.

Initially struggling with poor communication skills and shyness due to his Odia-medium schooling, Hara quickly adapted at KISS through effective teaching and mentoring. The supportive environment eliminated homesickness, making KISS a home away from home for him and other tribal children. The nutrition and healthcare facilities were also impressive.

Hara built friendships with students from various tribes, learning about their socio-cultural differences, which enriched his appreciation for diversity. After completing his studies, he worked with KISS as a District Coordinator in Rayagada, improving his financial and social standing. He later entered politics to serve his community, focusing on providing basic amenities, promoting education and healthcare, preserving culture and eradicating social evils.

Hara is passionate about sports, believing every tribal child is an enthusiast. KISS offers ample opportunities for students to excel in traditional and international games. As an ambassador of KISS, he aims to uplift his community, especially in education and health, encouraging KISS students to study hard and achieve their goals, recalling the founder's words, 'kana thili, kana heli, kana hebi' (What I was, what I became, and what I am going to be).

He also urges KISS alumni to stay connected with the KISS family, strengthening the institution and fostering pride among KISSians.

Ashok Muduli, Additional Tahasildar, Odisha Administrative Service, Revenue and Disaster Management Department, Government of Odisha

Ashok Muduli, born into the Paraja tribal community on 12 May 1992 in Raising village, Koraput, exemplifies the transformative power of KISS. Raised alongside five siblings in an environment of hardship, his father, a matriculate, worked as a contractual cook-cum-attendant at a school, while his illiterate mother supplemented the family's income as a farmhand.

Despite these challenges, Ashok's determination to learn remained strong. He attended a local primary school and later the Ekalavya Model Residential School in Pungar, Koraput. In 2006, he joined KISS as a +2 Science student and graduated with a BCA degree in 2012.

Through hard work, he qualified for the Odisha Administrative Service exam and is currently serving as an Additional Tahasildar in the Revenue and Disaster Management Department of the Government of Odisha. Ashok credits KISS with helping him achieve his dreams.

Initially aspiring to become a teacher, he found KISS to be a nurturing environment that helped him identify his strengths and weaknesses. Though he missed his old friends at first, he quickly formed new friendships and enjoyed supportive relationships with teachers, which eased his homesickness.

At KISS, Ashok maintained a connection to his cultural roots while embracing a new social life, making friends from across the state. He faced challenges with the English medium of instruction but overcame them through hard work and excellent academic support from cooperative teachers and weekly mentoring sessions.

Deeply connected to his tribal roots, Ashok engages with his community to discuss plans for its development. As a proud alumnus and brand ambassador of KISS, he is committed to uplifting his community. His message to KISS students and alumni is clear: 'The sky is the limit for every KISS student and alumnus; never give up until you reach your goals.'

Madhav Kemprai, Community Development, Assam

Madhav Kemprai hails from one of the remotest regions of Assam, called Dhansiri in Karbi Anglong district, an area that still lacks regular access to electricity, proper transportation and connectivity.

Madhav's family consists of four members: his mother, two younger brothers and himself. He lost his father, a petition writer in the notary office, to a heart attack when he was barely seven years old. This untimely loss threw his family into turmoil, both emotionally and economically, pushing them to the brink of poverty.

Madhav's mother struggled to earn a living to feed her three children and had to leave her youngest baby at Madhav's grandparents' home, about 50 km from their village. For a few years, the family struggled to provide two square meals a day, often borrowing food from neighbours for subsistence. After two years, the family began selling vegetables at a nearby local haat, which helped them make ends meet.

At the time of his father's passing, Madhav was in Class 1 at a private school in the region, while his younger siblings were not yet enrolled in school. However, due to financial constraints, Madhav was forced to switch schools and attend a government school. A year or two later, he was joined by his younger brother, and both completed their primary and middle schooling there.

Every winter, during those years, the boys would sell oranges on the roadside to earn money to pay for the forthcoming session's admission fees.

In 2005, an ethnic clash between two tribes of Karbi Anglong devastated the family further. As the family slept at night, a group of unidentified persons banged on the door, attempting to break in. Luckily, Madhav and his family sneaked out from the back door and were able to escape; others in their village were not as fortunate.

The Kemprai family walked nearly 10 km in the dark that night, finding their way amidst paddy fields and people's private properties until they were able to seek refuge at the house of Madhav's mother's friend in a neighbouring town.

The following morning, they boarded a passenger train and travelled to their maternal grandfather's home, from where the family went to the government relief camp for conflict victims. They lived in this camp for nearly four months until the conflict situation normalized. During this time, they received the sorrowful news that their house had been burnt and destroyed by unidentified goons.

After a few months, the government withdrew the relief camp, leaving the Kemprais and other families homeless, wandering around unsure of where to go or what to do. Luckily, they were able to purchase an area of forest land meant for the resettlement and rehabilitation of those affected by the ethnic conflict.

The group created a village called Dimaidi, around 30 km from their previous home, and settled there. Starting once again and without any capital, Madhav's mother struggled to sustain the family.

The family would collect wood from the forests for sale in the market, and this helped them earn their living till Madhav completed his Matric board examinations in 2008. At this point, his youngest brother rejoined the family, following the demise of the grandfather he had been raised by.

After graduating from Class 10, Madhav joined the +2 Science stream at Diphu Government College, about 27 km from his new house. There, he rented a room but was more worried about food and house rent expenses rather than his studies.

He began teaching some school children as a tutor, which unfortunately affected his own education, forcing him to drop out of school after passing Class 12. Fortunately, at this juncture, he was informed about KISS by the then President of the All Assam Dimasa Student Union. This knowledge completely transformed Madhav's future.

At KISS, Madhav completed his B.Sc. in Computer Science (2012–2014). His brother also pursued a +2 in Science (2011–2013), following which he cleared the medical competitive exam and received admission into an MBBS course at a government medical college in Assam.

After completing his B.Sc. from KISS, Madhav went on to pursue a postgraduate degree in Development Studies from Azim Premji University in Bangalore on a full scholarship. He is now pursuing a PhD from the Tata Institute of Social Sciences (TISS), Guwahati.

Madhav has also been involved with a grassroots NGO based in Bongaigaon district of Assam, working on community development programmes, particularly in the livelihoods sector with several vulnerable communities comprising both minorities and tribals from the region.

Madhav trained in archery during his time at KISS, under the supervision of Rajesh Hansdak, a renowned archery coach from Odisha. He represented KISS at the Inter-University Tournament conducted in 2011, in addition to participating in two state-level archery tournaments.

Madhav credits KISS's unique model of combining mental and physical education through sports for helping him develop critical thinking alongside understanding the world better.

In Madhav's own words: 'Without KISS, I would not have been able to complete my bachelor's degree, without which I definitely would not have been in the place where I am now. Similarly, my younger brother would not have been a doctor today had he not joined KISS. Now everybody can feel the happiness of the distressed mother when she finds both of her sons are highly educated and well-placed only because of KISS. I again would like to express my sincere gratitude to the Founder of KISS Dr Achyuta Samanta for teaching us how to fish and thereby enabling us to break the cycle of poverty.'

Sumitra Nayak, Captain, India Women's Rugby Team

Sumitra Nayak is the first Indian female nominated for the 2017 International Children's Peace Prize for her courage in advocating for children's rights. The prize, launched by KidsRights during the 2005 World Summit of Nobel Peace Laureates in Rome, is presented annually by a Nobel Peace laureate to young heroes.

Sumitra, the former captain of the girls' rugby team, has overcome numerous challenges, emerging as a trendsetter and achiever. She hails from a poor family in a remote village in the Jajpur district of Odisha. Her mother worked as a domestic maid, while her father was a daily wage labourer whose earnings often went towards alcohol.

From a young age, Sumitra faced financial hardship, domestic abuse, and the responsibility of caring for her two younger siblings. After enduring abuse from her father, her mother fled with her children, seeking refuge in Bhubaneswar with help from a former employer.

Sumitra joined KISS in 2008 in Class 4, marking the start of her transformative journey. She began practising rugby in 2009 and played in her first state match in 2012. Two years later, she participated in the U13 Women's Rugby World Cup and later took part in the National Championship and the National School Games. She helped her team win a bronze medal at the Asian Girls Rugby Sevens (U18) held in Dubai in 2016. Her love for rugby blossomed despite societal restrictions on girls in her village. With her mother's encouragement, she pursued her passion for the sport.

In 2018, Sumitra delivered a TED Talk in Pune, where she was introduced as 'a dreamer, achiever and trendsetter'. Her success story has inspired many children at KISS to follow her path. Fondly called Rugby Rani, Sumitra believes rugby has given her life meaning, stating, 'In fact, rugby is my life.' She aspires to become an IAS officer and envisions a world where every child grows up to be a change-maker, solving problems and building empathy.

Mamata Dalai, National Bravery Awardee

In 2018, six-year-old Mamata Dalai from Bankual village in Kendrapara district, Odisha, received the Bravery Award from Prime Minister Narendra Modi, which firmly placed her among the bravest young heroes of India.

On a fateful day in April 2017, Mamata and her

sister Asanti went to bathe in a pond near their house. A five-foot-long crocodile had strayed from a nearby river and suddenly attacked seven-year-old Asanti, clamping its jaws onto her right hand. Displaying remarkable bravery, Mamata fearlessly held onto her sister's left hand, refusing to let go. She pulled Asanti away and threw a utensil at the crocodile, causing it to release her sister and slip back into the water. The crocodile was later captured by forest officials from Bhitarkanika National Park.

Mamata's courageous act quickly garnered national attention. During the award ceremony, Prime Minister Modi praised her bravery and wished her a bright future. Mamata shared that he affectionately pulled her ear and encouraged her to pursue her dreams. Aspiring to become a doctor to serve her community, Mamata was admitted to KISS to continue her education.

Over the past seven years, KISS has provided Mamata with a supportive environment, enabling her to focus on her studies and personal development. She has excelled academically and participated in activities that developed her leadership skills and confidence.

Mamata's journey is a powerful reminder of the resilience of the human spirit and the impact of a nurturing educational environment. Her story has inspired many, demonstrating that courage and determination can overcome daunting obstacles. Motivated by her desire to give back to her community, Mamata continues to work hard toward her goal of becoming a doctor. Her success is a shining example of how access to quality education can transform lives.

Mamata's bravery not only saved her sister's life but also set her on a path to achieve her dreams and positively impact society. As she continues her journey at KISS, Mamata remains an inspiration, proving that with courage and support, anything is possible.

Shanti Murmu, Global Talent at UNLEASH 2022

Shanti Murmu, a Santal tribal woman from Indkholi village in the Mayurbhanj district of Odisha, has an inspiring life story marked by resilience. After losing her mother when she was just five months old, Shanti was raised by her paternal grandmother until the age of three. Her life became more challenging when her father remarried, and her stepmother treated her harshly.

Despite these difficulties, Shanti attended the village school, motivated by the hope of receiving a daily meal rather than a pure desire for education. She took on many responsibilities, such as caring for cattle and working in the fields on weekends. Her stepmother often discouraged her education by throwing her books away and denying her food.

A turning point came when Shanti joined Dumadihi High School, an SC/ST residential school in Rairangpur, where she excelled academically and completed her matriculation with high marks. With the support of her father, she enrolled in the +2 1st Year Science Class at KISS in 2013, while her family moved to a slum to support her education. The nurturing environment at KISS allowed Shanti to flourish, and her brothers later joined her there. At KISS, Shanti not only excelled academically but also engaged in various extracurricular activities like judo, vocational training and yoga. She became an active member of the debate group, Life Skills Education, KISS Youth Society and the Red Cross Society. Shanti's positive attitude and helpful nature inspired many, even leading to a change in her stepmother's behaviour.

In 2016, Shanti was selected as a member of the Ashoka Youth Venture for her initiative, 'Parivartan', becoming the first student from Odisha to receive this honour. Parivartan focuses on improving literacy, youth empowerment, and addressing social issues like menstrual health stigma, early marriage and alcoholism. Shanti's involvement extended beyond her community; she was a panellist discussing gender inequality with Laxmi Puri of UN Women in Delhi and shared her insights at the Shared Value Summit 2016 in Gurgaon.

She was also recognized as a Global Talent at UNLEASH 2022 and currently works with the Tata Steel Foundation, driving socio-economic change and empowering youth through her venture, Parivartan. Her relationship-building skills have been enhanced through fellowships, conferences and talks, establishing her as a well-rounded development professional. Shanti Murmu's story exemplifies resilience and commitment to bringing about positive change in society.

Hupi Majhi, International Rugby Player

When eight-year-old Hupi Majhi was sent to a boarding school in Bhubaneswar, she was filled with fear about what lay ahead. Growing up in the small village of Dhatika, north of Kendujhar District, Hupi was raised under strict customs that kept girls indoors as much as possible. Her only respite was the few hours she spent at school each day.

In 2005, Hupi joined KISS, where the initial weeks were challenging. She grappled with fear and found it difficult to interact with strangers. She recalls bunking classes due to her anxiety, going hungry because she was afraid to ask for more food, and struggling to communicate since she spoke Santhal, not Odia.

By 2017, Hupi had come a long way from the timid girl who first arrived at KISS. She transformed into a formidable rugby player, helping India achieve its best-ever finish at the Asia Rugby Women's Sevens Trophy in Vientiane, Laos, where she scored six tries, establishing herself as a key player.

Hupi's journey in sports began with athletics, where

she won inter-school meets in the 100m and 200m events, running barefoot. After a brief stint in cricket, she switched to rugby after watching foreign coaches at KISS, which sparked her interest in the sport that would change her life. Hupi made her international debut in early 2016 and became the top try scorer at several tournaments by 2017, including scoring 11 tries in five matches at the Asia Rugby Development Sevens Series.

Despite her small stature—standing at five feet and weighing just over 50 kg—her speed and agility set her apart. Coach Nasser Hussain praised her ability to read the game and identify spaces to exploit.

Reflecting on her journey, Hupi feels fortunate to have the opportunity to leave home and explore the world, unlike her elder sister, who was married at 18. Her brother-in-law's support was crucial in convincing her parents to send her to Bhubaneswar, where her athletic talent flourished.

As of 2024, Hupi has triggered a significant shift within her Santhal tribe in Dhatika. Her success has made her a role model, inspiring many, including juniors at KISS. She benefited from Odisha's robust sports policies, securing a government job and monetary rewards.

Hupi's transformation from a village girl confined indoors to an international rugby player is remarkable. She often sneaked out of her hut in the seventh grade to play rugby, a sport initially frowned upon in her community. Over time, her achievements sparked interest in rugby among villagers, changing their perception of the sport. Hupi Majhi's story is one of resilience and inspiration. Her achievements have brought recognition and altered societal norms in her village. As she continues to represent Odisha and India, she remains a beacon of hope for young girls, showing that, with determination and support, they too can overcome obstacles and achieve their dreams.

*Educating a girl child is equal to
educating generations thereafter.*

Dana Majhi and His Daughters: From Despair to Hope

In the remote village of Melaghar, located in the Thuamul-Rampur block of Odisha, lived Dana Majhi, a humble tribal man. Life there was harsh, and survival was a daily struggle. Dana's world was shattered when his wife, Amang Dei, succumbed to tuberculosis at the district headquarters hospital in Bhawanipatna. With no means of transportation, Dana had to carry his wife's lifeless body on his shoulders for 12 km back to their village, accompanied by his young daughter.

This heart-wrenching journey, made in the scorching heat, garnered global sympathy in 2017. The image of Dana's plight evoked a wave of empathy, prompting me to offer free education, food and accommodation to his three daughters: Chandini, Sonei and Pramila. Dana's story also reached the then Prime Minister of Bahrain, who was deeply moved and donated ₹9 lakh to support the family. This generous gift was deposited as fixed deposits in the names of Dana's daughters, ensuring their financial security.

Chandini, Sonei and Pramila were enrolled at KISS in Bhubaneswar, where they found not only education but also a nurturing environment that fostered their growth. Their transition was remarkable; from a life of uncertainty, they now had the promise of a brighter future. Chandini, the eldest, despite her traumatic past, scored 280 out of 600 marks in her matriculation exam.

Life at KISS profoundly changed the sisters' lives,

providing them with opportunities and encouragement. They expressed their joy and sense of belonging, stating that they no longer wished to return to their native village, having found security and hope. The impact of Dana Majhi's story extended beyond his family. Villagers in Kalahandi, who had watched Dana's journey, now saw a glimmer of hope. KISS's intervention not only changed the lives of the girls but also inspired the community to believe in the power of education.

Dana's story has become a symbol of resilience and transformation. With KISS's continuous support, his daughters were on a path to a promising future. Their journey from hardship to opportunity served as inspiration for many other tribal children, highlighting the importance of compassion, support and education in breaking the cycle of poverty.

Dr Saunri Hansdah, Gynaecologist, Government Medical College

Saunri Hansdah, a Santhal girl from Jugalkishorepur in Keonjhar district, is a first-generation learner and the first child in her family to receive an education, as her parents recognized the power of education and were committed to ensuring opportunities for their children.

Saunri began her journey at KISS when she enrolled in Class 12 in 2007. She quickly adapted and excelled in her +2 science examinations, leading to further educational opportunities. Her academic success earned her a place at KIMS, where she pursued an MBBS degree. By 2017, she was in her final year, dedicated to becoming a doctor.

Saunri graduated with her MBBS, marking a significant milestone for her and her community. Currently specializing in gynaecology after qualifying for the NEET-PG examination, Saunri is committed to using her skills to serve her community.

She plans to work with Primary Health Centres in her district to combat superstitious health beliefs prevalent in tribal society. By providing accurate medical information and accessible healthcare, she aims to eradicate these harmful practices.

Saunri is also passionate about inspiring other children in her community to pursue education. She frequently returns to her village to engage in activities that support her community. Drawing immense inspiration from KISS and its commitment to marginalized communities, Saunri feels fortunate to have been part of such a nurturing environment. Her journey and achievements are a source of pride for her family, community and KISS. As she continues to serve and inspire others, Saunri exemplifies the profound impact that education and support can have in changing lives and creating a brighter future for all.

Jadhu Mallik, Organic Farmer

'What is the price of this heap of wood you are going to sell at the market today?' Jadhu (name changed for anonymity) asked curiously as he watched his parents lift the bundle onto their heads and head towards the village market.

'₹10 for this pile,' his father replied.

'Please sell it for ₹100 today,' Jadhu insisted, shocked and surprised at the same time.

'Na. Nobody buys at that rate. You know how much ₹100 is?'

'Of course. But for me, sell it for ₹100 and see. Just for today.'

Jadhu somehow convinced his parents to sell the wood at ten times their usual price. To their astonishment, it sold quickly at the nearby market.

When his father asked for an explanation, Jadhu revealed,

'It is sandalwood. It can be sold at ₹1,000. I said ₹100 because you would never have agreed to ₹1,000.'

Jadhu's father, knowledgeable about forest produce but unaware of pricing dynamics, was dumbfounded but deeply satisfied that he had sent his only son to KISS in Bhubaneswar. There, Jadhu received an education that empowered him with knowledge beyond their village's limited grasp. Had he attended a nearby school, he might have dropped out or remained uninformed about the world. That day, his father realized the profound importance of education for their vulnerable tribal community, seeing it as a means to break intergenerational poverty and allow indigenous knowledge to flourish when combined with formal education. Moved by this realization, he decided to send his daughter to KISS as well.

Countless stories like Jadhu's exist at KISS, which offers a new lease on life to students who are proud of their tribal culture and identity. KISS has become synonymous with transformative economic, social, political and psychological empowerment through holistic, quality education. The institution stems from my passion and commitment to ensuring that no child endures what I once did.

My experiences of poverty, hunger and humiliation fuelled my resolve to create a space where disadvantaged children can access quality education, leading to the establishment of KIIT and KISS, which took on the responsibility of providing free, quality education to vulnerable children. Starting KIIT and KISS was challenging. Its success required immense hard work. The struggles I faced in the first 10 years were formidable, with daily battles against the urge to give up. With just ₹5,000, I started KIIT, which has now grown into an institution that serves as a case study for management graduates. Without KISS, thousands of tribal children would have remained isolated or fallen into traps like violent extremism, early marriage, or harassment.

My life's work focuses on social empowerment and upliftment, creating change leaders who can carry forward my mission. My only ambition is to bring smiles to the faces of young children—the empowered citizens of tomorrow. Visitors to KIIT and KISS often express amazement at our achievements in various sectors, recommending me for awards, many of which I scarcely know about. For instance, a jurist from the USA once recommended me for the ISA Award for Service to Humanity and the highest civilian award from Bahrain, worth USD one million.

While I've received many accolades, my inspiration comes from the lives we transform. Every child who finds hope at KISS is my true reward. I am heartened that our work is visible and recognized, inspiring others to take up similar humanitarian efforts. Despite these achievements, I live a simple life. I often say with a smile, 'One should not forget the roots from which one comes. One should also ensure that the present and future are shaped with commitment and resolve.'

The Art of Giving and KISS are intertwined, demonstrating how education and compassion can transform lives. This philosophy has touched millions, bringing profound changes and offering new hope and opportunities. These stories highlight the impact of our work, showing how the Art of Giving has changed lives for the better, one child at a time.

10

A Practical Guide to Practise the Art of Giving

IN THE JOURNEY OF LIFE, ACTS OF GIVING AND SHARING bring unparalleled joy and satisfaction. The philosophy of the Art of Giving is not merely a concept but a way of life that enriches both the giver and the recipient. The goal of this chapter is to guide readers through practical steps to incorporate the Art of Giving into their daily lives, making it a natural extension of their being.

Introduction

The Art of Giving transcends cultural, religious and personal boundaries, emphasizing the joy of giving without expecting anything in return. This principle has the power to transform lives by fostering an environment of mutual respect and care, enabling a life filled with generosity and kindness.

Understanding the Core Principles

At its heart, the Art of Giving is about selflessness and generosity. True happiness doesn't stem from what we receive, but from what we give. The benefits of such actions are profound, impacting not only those who receive them but also enriching our own lives. Psychological research supports this, showing that giving can enhance mental health, strengthen social connections and even boost physical well-being.

Self-assessment

To begin, it is essential to reflect on one's current giving habits. Consider how often you help others, the nature of your contributions and your motivations. This self-assessment can be eye-opening, revealing strengths and areas where you can enhance your giving practices.

Small Beginnings

Starting small is key to making giving a regular part of life. It can be as simple as offering a compliment, giving up your seat for someone, or spending time with elderly neighbours. Each small act of kindness gradually makes giving an instinctive and fulfilling habit.

Developing a Giving Mindset

Cultivating a mindset that prioritizes giving over receiving requires conscious effort. It involves practising gratitude and recognizing the abundance in your life, which, in turn, fosters generosity. Daily habits such as reflecting on moments of giving or keeping a journal of kind acts can help reinforce this mindset.

Giving in Everyday Life

Incorporating giving into your daily routine can be effortless yet meaningful. This might include offering emotional support to a friend, sharing resources with someone in need or volunteering your skills. The key is to remain mindful of opportunities where even small contributions can create a significant impact.

Volunteering

Volunteering is one of the most impactful ways to practise the Art of Giving. Whether helping at a local food bank, teaching underprivileged children or assisting senior citizens, volunteering allows you to contribute directly to others' well-being. Choosing causes that resonate with you makes the experience even more fulfilling.

Financial Giving

While giving time and effort is invaluable, financial giving also plays a vital role. It is important to donate responsibly, ensuring that your contributions are used effectively. Researching charities, understanding their impact and supporting organizations with transparent practices can maximize the value of your donations.

Giving at the Workplace

The workplace offers a unique platform for promoting the Art of Giving. Initiating or participating in giving programmes not only benefits society but also fosters a culture of generosity and team spirit among employees. Activities like charity drives, corporate matching gifts, or community service days can significantly boost workplace morale.

Advanced Giving: Starting Initiatives

For those inspired to take their giving to the next level, starting a community initiative can be a transformative experience. This involves identifying a need, gathering support and mobilizing resources to create a tangible impact.

Engaging the community and building a dedicated team can amplify your efforts, leading to sustainable change.

Measuring Impact to Ensure One's Contributions Make a Difference

Measuring the impact of your giving is essential for understanding its effectiveness and guiding future efforts. It brings transparency and accountability while offering valuable insights that can inspire further action.

Establish Clear Objectives: Before measuring impact, define your goals. Are you aiming to improve education, reduce poverty, enhance community health or bring comfort to the elderly? Clear objectives help you assess whether your efforts are meeting their intended targets.

Develop Indicators: Identify tangible indicators to measure success. For example, if your objective is to improve education in a community, indicators could include the number of students graduating, improved test scores, or increased attendance rates.

Analyse and Reflect: Regularly assess the effectiveness of your giving by analysing data and seeking feedback. Look for patterns or trends that highlight successes or reveal areas needing improvement. Reflecting with your team or community members offers diverse perspectives and valuable insights.

Long-term Tracking: Impact measurement should be an ongoing process, not a one-time activity. Tracking results over time reveals not just immediate outcomes but also long-term changes. This helps you see how sustained efforts lead to meaningful and lasting transformations.

By systematically measuring the impact of your giving, you ensure that your efforts are not only heartfelt but also effective. This process enhances the benefits for recipients and deepens your own experience of giving. It provides a clearer path towards fulfilling your philanthropic goals while inspiring others to join you in spreading kindness and compassion.

11

Impact of the Art of Giving on its Practitioners

What Happens if One Practises the Art of Giving

The Art of Giving goes beyond the mere act of transferring material possessions to someone in need. It embodies a profound and multifaceted practice that touches various aspects of human existence, encompassing psychological, emotional, social and ethical dimensions. Celebrated across cultures and societies, the act of giving is revered for its transformative effects on both individuals and communities. This chapter explores the wide-ranging impact of the Art of Giving, examining its benefits at the micro level for individuals and at the macro level for society.

MICRO-LEVEL IMPACT: TRANSFORMATIVE EFFECTS ON INDIVIDUALS

Enhancing Happiness and Well-being

Giving profoundly enhances individual happiness and overall well-being. Numerous psychological studies have shown that acts of generosity trigger what is often referred to as a 'helper's high'—a feeling of euphoria followed by prolonged emotional well-being. This occurs due to the release of endorphins, the brain's natural painkillers and mood enhancers. For instance, a Harvard Business School study found that individuals who spent money on others reported greater happiness than those who spent it on themselves.[2] This effect is not limited to financial giving; time and effort spent helping others also contribute to this elevated state of happiness.

Reducing Stress and Anxiety

Practising the Art of Giving can significantly reduce stress and anxiety. When individuals focus on the needs of others, they often experience a shift in perspective, alleviating their own worries. This redirection of focus lowers cortisol levels, the hormone associated with stress. Additionally, giving fosters a sense of purpose and fulfilment, mitigating feelings of anxiety and depression. Research published in *Health Psychology* revealed that individuals engaged in volunteer activities had lower blood pressure and reported reduced stress levels.[3]

Fostering Empathy and Compassion

Giving nurtures empathy and compassion, essential qualities for emotional intelligence and healthy interpersonal relationships. Engaging in acts of generosity helps individuals develop a deeper sensitivity to the struggles and needs of

[2]Dunn, Elizabeth W., Lara B. Aknin, and Michael I. Norton, 'Spending Money on Others Promotes Happiness', *Science* 319, no. 5870, 21 March 2008, pp. 1687–1688.

[3]Sneed, Rodlescia S., and Sheldon Cohen, 'A Prospective Study of Volunteerism and Hypertension Risk in Older Adults', *Psychology and Aging*, vol. 28, no. 2, June 2013, pp. 578–86. https://doi.org/10.1037/a0032718. Accessed on 25 March 2025.

others. This empathetic outlook strengthens social bonds, fostering more meaningful and supportive relationships. Educational initiatives like Canada's 'Roots of Empathy' programme, where babies and their parents are brought into classrooms to help children understand and connect with others' emotions, highlight how consistent exposure to giving cultivates empathy and compassion.

Strengthening Character and Integrity

The Art of Giving plays a crucial role in shaping moral and ethical values. Acts of generosity encourage individuals to act from a sense of duty and righteousness rather than personal gain, fostering integrity and character. By making giving a regular practice, individuals develop a strong moral compass that guides their actions and decisions.

Philanthropists like Andrew Carnegie exemplified this by using their fortunes to promote the greater good.[4] Carnegie's contributions to public libraries and educational institutions reflect how giving, rooted in ethical responsibility, promotes integrity and social accountability.

Promoting Selflessness and Altruism

Giving cultivates selflessness and altruism, shifting the focus from self-centred desires to the well-being of others. This perspective enhances life's meaning and fulfilment, as individuals find joy in helping others. Acts of selflessness strengthen social bonds and foster a more compassionate and cohesive society. An inspiring example is Oseola

---

[4]'Andrew Carnegie's Library Legacy: A Timeline', *Carnegie Corporation of New York*, www.carnegie.org/our-work/article/andrew-carnegies-library-legacy. Accessed on 25 March 2025.

McCarty, a washerwoman who donated her life savings to fund scholarships for students in need.[5] Her altruism, despite her modest means, demonstrates how giving can create a lasting impact.

Enhancing Cognitive Function and Creativity

Acts of giving can also stimulate cognitive functions and creativity. When individuals think of ways to help others, they engage in problem-solving and innovative thinking. This mental exercise enhances agility and creativity, contributing to intellectual growth.

Moreover, interacting with diverse groups while giving broadens one's perspective, fostering open-mindedness and adaptability. For instance, social enterprises like TOMS Shoes, which donates a pair of shoes for every pair sold, showcase how creative problem-solving can emerge from a commitment to giving.[6]

Fostering a Growth Mindset

The Art of Giving promotes a growth mindset—the belief that abilities and intelligence can be developed through dedication and hard work. Focusing on the positive impact of their actions fosters resilience and perseverance in individuals. A growth mindset encourages them to embrace challenges and view failures as opportunities for

---

[5]Alexander, Samantha McCain, APR, 'Oseola McCarty's Legacy of Generosity Reaches $1 Million Milestone', *The University of Southern Mississippi*, www.usm.edu/news/2025/release/oseola-mccarty.php. Accessed on 25 March 2025.

[6]Naeini, Arezou, et al., 'Case Study: How TOMS Shoes Made a Cause the Centre of Its Activities', *Business Today*, 28 May 2015, https://shorturl.at/D40uX. Accessed on 25 March 2025.

learning and self-improvement.[7] This concept, popularized by psychologist Carol Dweck, aligns with giving, as acts of generosity build mental strength, adaptability and a willingness to learn from experiences.

MACRO-LEVEL IMPACT: TRANSFORMATIVE EFFECTS ON SOCIETY

Enhancing Social Cohesion and Solidarity

Generosity plays a vital role in building stronger, more cohesive communities. When individuals give—whether through time, resources or support—they contribute to the overall well-being and resilience of their communities. This collective generosity fosters a sense of belonging and mutual support, strengthening social bonds. By creating networks of care, acts of giving promote community solidarity, enabling groups to effectively address challenges and support their members. Initiatives such as neighbourhood watch programmes or community gardens exemplify how collective giving enhances cohesion, fostering shared responsibility and trust.

Promoting Social Capital and Trust

The Art of Giving contributes to the development of social capital—the networks, norms, and trust that facilitate cooperation and collaboration within communities. High levels of social capital are associated with improved public health, economic prosperity and social stability. Acts of generosity build trust and reciprocity, creating a virtuous

---

[7]Dweck, Carol S., *Mindset: How You Can Fulfil Your Potential*, Robinson Books, 2012.

cycle of giving and mutual support. This trust fosters collaboration, enabling communities to work towards shared goals. Sociologist Robert Putnam described social capital as being built through networks of trust and reciprocity.[8] Programmes like Time Banks, where community members exchange services based on time rather than money, illustrate how giving strengthens social capital.

Addressing Economic Disparities

Giving plays a significant role in reducing economic disparities and promoting social justice. By redistributing resources and opportunities, acts of generosity contribute to a more equitable society. Philanthropic efforts, such as donations to education, healthcare and social services, provide essential support to disadvantaged groups and foster upward mobility. These contributions improve access to services, creating opportunities and reducing inequality. For instance, the Gates Foundation funds initiatives that provide vaccines, enhance education and support economic development in underserved regions, significantly addressing global disparities.

Empowering Marginalized Communities

Generosity empowers marginalized communities by providing them with the resources and support they need to thrive. Community-driven initiatives and grassroots organizations often rely on donations and volunteerism to fund their programmes. By supporting these initiatives, donors amplify the voices of marginalized groups and promote social

---

[8]Putnam, R. D., *Making Democracy Work: Civic Traditions in Modern Italy*, Princeton University Press, 1993.

inclusion. This empowerment fosters a more equitable society where individuals from all backgrounds have the opportunity to succeed. Organizations like Kiva, which offer microloans to entrepreneurs in developing countries, illustrate this impact. These small loans enable individuals to start or expand businesses, driving economic and social mobility.

Inspiring Collective Action

Generosity is contagious—it begets generosity. When individuals witness acts of giving, they are often inspired to follow suit, creating a ripple effect of kindness and compassion. This culture of generosity can transform societies, making them more compassionate and united. Public recognition of philanthropic efforts and stories of impactful giving motivates others to contribute.

For example, the Ice Bucket Challenge, which raised awareness and funds for ALS (amyotrophic lateral sclerosis) research, exemplifies how acts of giving can inspire global collective action. The campaign went viral, encouraging millions to participate, generating significant donations and fostering a worldwide spirit of generosity.

Promoting Civic Engagement and Volunteerism

The Art of Giving often encourages civic engagement and volunteerism. By participating in community service, individuals contribute to the common good and strengthen their communities.

Volunteering fosters civic responsibility and active citizenship, encouraging individuals to address community needs. This engagement leads to more vibrant and dynamic communities, where people work together for positive change. Programmes like AmeriCorps and the Peace Corps promote volunteerism by inspiring individuals to dedicate time and skills to service, fostering a sense of active citizenship.[9]

Leaving a Lasting Impact

Acts of generosity often leave a lasting impact on both the giver and the recipient. This impact can manifest as improved well-being, strengthened relationships and a more just society. Supporting long-term initiatives and sustainable projects creates enduring positive change, benefiting future generations. For example, the Rockefeller Foundation, established over a century ago, continues to influence public health, education and scientific research, leaving a legacy of progress. Similarly, Carnegie Libraries, funded by Andrew Carnegie, have provided access to education and knowledge for millions, inspiring individuals to pursue learning and contribute to their communities.

Creating a Legacy of Kindness

Generosity can create a legacy of kindness that transcends generations. By modelling and teaching the importance of giving, individuals inspire future generations to continue this tradition. Educational programmes and family practices that emphasize generosity instil a sense of social responsibility and compassion in young people. This legacy fosters a more empathetic and altruistic society, where individuals prioritize the well-being of others.

---

[9]Gagliardi, Pietro, et al., 'Promoting Youth Volunteering and Civic Service Engagement', *OECD Working Papers on Public Governance*, 5 Dec 2024, https://doi.org/10.1787/39659e6a-en. Accessed on 25 March 2025.

Personal Transformation and Fulfilment

Ultimately, practising the Art of Giving transforms the giver, leading to a deeper sense of fulfilment and purpose. By focusing on the welfare of others, individuals find greater meaning in their own lives. The act of giving fosters personal growth, helping individuals cultivate virtues such as empathy, compassion and selflessness. This transformation enhances their overall well-being, fostering a more harmonious and balanced life.

POWER OF GIVING: GIVING MAKES US FEEL HAPPY

Research consistently shows that generosity boosts happiness and well-being. A 2008 study by Harvard Business School Professor Michael Norton and his colleagues found that participants who gave money to others experienced greater happiness than those who spent it on themselves.[10] Similarly, Sonja Lyubomirsky, a psychology professor at the University of California, Riverside, observed that people who performed five acts of kindness each week for six weeks reported increased happiness.[11]

These positive effects are also reflected biologically. A 2006 study by Jorge Moll and colleagues at the National Institutes of Health found that giving to charities activates regions of the brain associated with pleasure, social connection

---

[10]Dunn, Elizabeth W., Lara B. Aknin, and Michael I. Norton, 'Spending Money on Others Promotes Happiness', *Science* 319, no. 5870, 21 March 2008, pp. 1687–1688.

[11]Lyubomirsky, Sonja, et al., *Pursuing Sustained Happiness Through Random Acts of Kindness and Counting One's Blessings: Tests of Two Six-Week Interventions*, Unpublished raw data, 2004, doi:10.1037/1089-2680.9.2.111. Accessed on 25 March 2025.

and trust, creating a 'warm glow' effect.[12] The Akshaya Patra Foundation, an NGO in India, provides mid-day meals to millions of schoolchildren. Volunteers and donors frequently report profound happiness and fulfilment from their contributions. Many corporate employees who participate in meal distribution events express joy and satisfaction from witnessing the immediate impact of their giving on the children's faces. This sense of happiness aligns with studies indicating that giving enhances personal well-being.

Giving is Good for Our Health

Numerous studies have linked generosity to better health outcomes, even among the sick and elderly. In his book *Why Good Things Happen to Good People*, Stephen Post, a professor of preventive medicine at Stony Brook University, reports that giving to others increases health benefits in people with chronic illnesses, including HIV and multiple sclerosis.

A 1999 study led by Doug Oman of the University of California, Berkeley, found that elderly people who volunteered for two or more organizations were 44 per cent less likely to die over a five-year period than non-volunteers, even after controlling for age, exercise habits and general health.[13] Similarly, Stephanie Brown of the University of Michigan found in a 2003 study that elderly couples who provided practical help to friends, relatives or neighbours—or gave

---

[12]Moll, Jorge, et al., 'Human Fronto–mesolimbic Networks Guide Decisions About Charitable Donation', *Proceedings of the National Academy of Sciences*, vol. 103, no. 42, October 2006, pp. 15623–28. https://doi.org/10.1073/pnas.0604475103. Accessed on 25 March 2025.

[13]Oman, Doug, et al., 'Volunteerism and Mortality Among the Community-dwelling Elderly', *Journal of Health Psychology*, vol. 4, no. 3, May 1999, pp. 301–16. https://doi.org/10.1177/135910539900400301. Accessed on 25 March 2025.

emotional support to their spouses—had a lower risk of dying over a five-year period than those who did not. Interestingly, receiving help was not linked to reduced mortality risk.[14]

Researchers suggest that giving may improve physical health and longevity by reducing stress, which is associated with various health issues.[15] Initiatives like Daan Utsav, also known as the 'Joy of Giving Week', celebrated annually in India from 2 to 8 October, reflect this spirit of generosity. During this week, people from all walks of life engage in acts of giving, including donations, volunteering and charity events. Participants frequently share how these activities bring them immense joy and a sense of purpose, demonstrating how communal generosity uplifts both the givers and recipients.

Giving Promotes Cooperation and Social Connection

Generosity fosters cooperation and strengthens social bonds. Studies by sociologists Brent Simpson and Robb Willer show that when individuals give, they are more likely to receive generosity in return—sometimes from the same person and sometimes from others.[16] This reciprocity promotes trust and cooperation, reinforcing social ties.

---

[14]Brown, Stephanie L., et al., 'Providing Social Support May Be More Beneficial Than Receiving It', *Psychological Science*, vol. 14, no. 4, June 2003, pp. 320–27. https://doi.org/10.1111/1467-9280.14461. Accessed on 25 March 2025.

[15]Poulin, Michael J., et al., 'Giving to Others and the Association Between Stress and Mortality', *American Journal of Public Health*, vol. 103, no. 9, January 2013, pp. 1649–55. https://doi.org/10.2105/ajph.2012.300876. Accessed on 25 March 2025.

[16]Simpson, Brent, and Robb Willer, 'Beyond Altruism: Sociological Foundations of Cooperation and Prosocial Behavior', *Annual Review of Sociology*, vol. 41, no. 1, May 2015, pp. 43–63. https://doi.org/10.1146/annurev-soc-073014-112242. Accessed on 25 March 2025.

Positive social interactions fuelled by generosity are essential for mental and physical well-being. In his book *Loneliness: Human Nature and the Need for Social Connection*, John Cacioppo notes, 'The more extensive the reciprocal altruism born of social connection...the greater the advance towards health, wealth, and happiness.'

When we give, we not only make others feel closer to us but also feel closer to them. Lyubomirsky, in *The How of Happiness*, writes, 'Being kind and generous leads you to perceive others more positively and more charitably,' which, she explains, 'fosters a heightened sense of interdependence and cooperation in your social community.'

The ISKCON Food Relief Foundation's Annamrita programme illustrates this principle. Volunteers, many of whom are elderly, prepare and distribute meals to underprivileged children. Anecdotal evidence suggests that these elderly volunteers experience improved physical and mental health, reduced loneliness and a renewed sense of purpose through their involvement.

Giving Evokes Gratitude

Generosity also evokes gratitude—whether you are on the giving or receiving end. Receiving a gift often elicits gratitude, while giving is a way of expressing it. Research has shown that gratitude is linked to greater happiness, better health and stronger social bonds.[17]

Robert Emmons and Michael McCullough, co-directors of the Research Project on Gratitude and Thankfulness, found that college students who regularly 'counted their blessings'

---

[17]Hill, Patrick L., et al., 'Examining the Pathways Between Gratitude and Self-rated Physical Health Across Adulthood', *Personality and Individual Differences*, vol. 54, no. 1, September 2012, pp. 92–96. https://doi.org/10.1016/j.paid.2012.08.011. Accessed on 25 March 2025.

exercised more, felt more optimistic, and reported higher overall life satisfaction.[18] Similarly, a study led by Nathaniel Lambert at Florida State University found that expressing gratitude to close friends or romantic partners strengthens emotional connections.[19]

Barbara Fredrickson, a leading happiness researcher, argues in her book *Positivity*: 'When you express your gratitude in words or actions, you not only boost your own positivity but [other people's] as well.' She adds, 'And in the process you reinforce their kindness and strengthen your bond to one another.'

Many Indian corporations promote this through corporate social responsibility programmes. For instance, Tata Group encourages employees to volunteer for educational and environmental projects, fostering teamwork and connection with local communities. Employees often develop lasting relationships with the people they help, creating more cohesive societies.

Giving is Contagious

Generosity also has a ripple effect, inspiring others to give. A study by James Fowler of the University of California, San Diego, and Nicholas Christakis of Harvard University, published in the *Proceedings of the National Academy of Sciences*, found that when one person behaves generously, it inspires observers to act generously towards others. This ripple effect can extend up to three degrees—from person to person to

[18]McCullough, Michael E., et al., 'Is Gratitude a Moral Affect?', *Psychological Bulletin*, vol. 127, no. 2, March 2001, pp. 249–66. https://doi.org/10.1037/0033-2909.127.2.249. Accessed on 25 March 2025.

[19]Lambert, Nathaniel M., et al., 'Benefits of Expressing Gratitude', *Psychological Science*, vol. 21, no. 4, March 2010, pp. 574–80. https://doi.org/10.1177/0956797610364003. Accessed on 25 March 2025.

person. 'As a result,' they write, 'each person in a network can influence dozens or even hundreds of people, some of whom [they do] not know and [have] not met.'[20]

Generosity is also associated with the release of oxytocin, a hormone linked to warmth, euphoria and social connection. Laboratory studies by Paul Zak, director of the Center for Neuroeconomics Studies at Claremont Graduate University, show that oxytocin enhances empathy and generosity, with its effects lasting for up to two hours.[21] This hormonal response can strengthen social bonds and ignite further generosity, creating a cascade of kindness throughout communities.

WHY DO WE GIVE?

Our predisposition to giving appears to be deeply rooted in evolution. Compared to other animals, humans spend an extended period developing from infants to toddlers to children capable of fending for themselves. During these vulnerable stages, survival depends heavily on support from family and the broader community. This prolonged dependence has likely hardwired humans to care for the vulnerable, making generosity a fundamental part of our nature.

But does this instinct for compassion conflict with Charles Darwin's theory of 'survival of the fittest'? Not necessarily. In *The Descent of Man*, Darwin described humans as highly social creatures with an 'almost ever-present instinct of

---

[20]Fowler, James H., and Nicholas A. Christakis, 'Cooperative Behavior Cascades in Human Social Networks', *Proceedings of the National Academy of Sciences*, vol. 107, no. 12, March 2010, pp. 5334–38. https://doi.org/10.1073/pnas.0913149107. Accessed on 25 March 2025.

[21]Zak, Paul J., et al., 'Oxytocin Increases Generosity in Humans', *PLoS ONE*, vol. 2, no. 11, November 2007, p. e1128. https://doi.org/10.1371/journal.pone.0001128. Accessed on 25 March 2025.

sympathy'—a trait acquired over time 'for the good of the community'. More recently, scientists have proposed the concept of group selection, suggesting that natural selection operates not only at the individual level but also at the group level. According to this framework, groups in which members occasionally sacrifice for one another are more likely to thrive and survive. Thus, generosity may have evolved as an adaptive advantage that strengthens group cohesion and resilience.

The Transformative Power of Giving

Acts of generosity have the remarkable ability to transform the heart and mind, often shifting individuals from negative or indifferent mindsets to more positive and compassionate ones. This internal shift fosters a deep sense of joy, fulfilment and satisfaction.

For instance, individuals who once viewed others' needs with apathy or scepticism may, through regular acts of giving, develop a more empathetic and compassionate outlook. This transformation goes beyond actions—it redefines core beliefs and attitudes, making individuals more attuned to the experiences and struggles of others.

Giving Nurtures Kindness and Empathy

Generosity fosters emotional, cognitive and behavioural changes. It encourages individuals to shift from self-centredness towards a more empathetic and inclusive worldview. By seeing the world through others' eyes, people become more aware of shared human experiences, recognizing both the joys and struggles faced by others. This broader perspective deepens empathy and strengthens the sense of interconnectedness.

As people become more mindful of others' needs, they naturally develop a greater inclination towards altruism. They may find themselves more willing to lend a helping hand, share resources and offer support to those around them. This creates a positive feedback loop, reinforcing their compassionate instincts.

The Personal Rewards of Giving

The benefits of giving extend beyond helping others—it also offers profound personal rewards. Engaging in selfless acts has been shown to:

- **Increase happiness**: Giving triggers the brain's pleasure and reward centres, creating a sense of joy and satisfaction.
- **Reduce stress**: Acts of kindness offer a sense of control and accomplishment, helping individuals cope with their own challenges. Assisting others can also put personal struggles into perspective, making them seem more manageable.
- **Enhance purpose and fulfilment**: Knowing that one's actions are making a positive impact fosters a deeper sense of purpose, often lacking in other areas of life.

Spreading Positivity through Generosity

The transformative power of giving lies in its capacity to inspire profound emotional and psychological growth. It helps individuals shift from pessimism to optimism, promotes emotional and mental well-being, and nurtures the development of kinder, more compassionate individuals.

Moreover, giving creates a ripple effect, spreading positivity far beyond the individual. Acts of generosity can inspire others to follow suit, fostering a more empathetic, compassionate and connected global community. By embracing generosity, individuals can catalyse waves of kindness that extend far beyond themselves, making the world a better place, one selfless act at a time.

12

Concluding Thoughts

I UNKNOWINGLY EMBARKED ON A JOURNEY OF SIGNIFICANT accomplishment—one that has shaped countless lives and left an enduring impact on society. Any such journey that influences the course of history inevitably raises questions about the means employed to achieve its ends. People often ask about the 'how', 'when', 'what' and 'where' of these achievements.

The stories of Vasco da Gama, who reached India, and Christopher Columbus, who discovered America, offer fitting parallels. Both explorers achieved monumental feats with limited resources and no clear directions. Lacking detailed maps or guaranteed routes to success, they were guided primarily by their determination and vision.

In my own journey with KIIT and KISS, I find a deep similarity with these historical voyages. Just as these explorers set out with scant means but unwavering resolve, I, too, began with virtually nothing in hand. What I lacked in material resources, I compensated for with passion, dedication and unyielding faith.

The inception of KIIT and KISS was not the result of abundant resources but of struggles, sacrifices and a willingness to take risks. The path was fraught with challenges. With no significant financial backing or influential connections, the journey was driven by a singular purpose: to make a difference and create something of lasting value for society. These institutions began as humble ideas, rooted in a dream to bring educational and social change to Odisha—a state often overlooked and underestimated in its potential for academic excellence and social transformation. What started in a small, rented space has grown into globally recognised educational hubs, a testament to the power of unwavering resolve and the manifestation of divine grace.

Throughout this journey, I have drawn strength from the belief that a higher power guides and supports our endeavours. This faith has been my constant source of inspiration and resilience, enabling me to overcome obstacles and stay committed to the mission.

The impact of KIIT and KISS extends far beyond academia. These institutions have become catalysts for social change, significantly contributing to the socio-economic development of Odisha and India. Through education and empowerment, they have uplifted marginalized communities, offering hope and opportunity where it was once scarce.

Looking ahead, the journey of KIIT and KISS is far from over. The vision is to continue on this path of consolidation, growth and service. Like the explorers who opened new worlds, KIIT and KISS will continue to blaze new trails in education and social service, expanding their reach and deepening their impact. This journey is underpinned by divine support and a profound connection to the land and people of Odisha. It remains a source of inspiration and transformation, creating a lasting legacy in the hearts and souls of everyone it touches.

I will serve society selflessly. Society has made me what I am. I will pay back the debt, without being complacent.

What Spiritual Leaders Have to Say

'I have been profoundly touched during my visits to KISS, and I feel that the voice India's tribal community is here. Dr Samanta and his KIIT and KISS are examples of compassion in action.'

—His Holiness Gyetrul Jigme Rinpoche
Master of Tibetan Buddhism and
Spiritual Director of Ripa International Center

'If you truly want to rise in life, pursuing a selfish agenda can only take you so far. However, if you expand outward and include others—ensuring that your actions benefit more and more people—you will rise without limit. Your founder [Dr Samanta] is one such example. The more we think of others, work for others, and serve others, the more fulfilled and happy we become. I asked Dr Samanta, "With the life you are leading and what you are doing, do you feel you are sacrificing?" He replied, "Not at all. I have got more than anyone else. I am the happiest person."

You see, the more you do for others, the more you think of others, the happier you will be—automatically, immediately, and lastingly. Think about it: anything we do for ourselves, we may forget or regret later. But the little that you do for someone else, you will never regret. You will always be happy. Whatever happens in life, you can at least say that you did something for somebody else without any thought of return.

It is deeply satisfying—this ideal of selflessness and Seva. In Sanskrit, we have three words: Shraddha—which means faith in yourself, faith in others, and faith in your culture and religion; Dhyan—which means attention and concentration, not distraction; and Seva—which means service. These three concepts converge in Dr Samanta.'

—Swami Sarvapriyananda
Minister and Spiritual Leader,
Vedanta Society of New York

'My gratitude goes to Dr Samanta, who is a remarkable figure of inspiration. I don't think anyone would deny that his story is profoundly inspiring. He may not wear the same cloth as I do, but he lives by its principles. He believes in the power of God but does not preach it. He is constantly working to uplift others and add value to their lives.

Having 80,000 students at the Kalinga Institute of Social Sciences (KISS) and 40,000 at the Kalinga Institute of Industrial Technology (KIIT) is an incredible achievement in just 25 years. We must applaud that. The value he adds to the lives of these children from tribal communities is absolutely amazing.'

—Prabhu Gaur Gopal Das
Life Coach and Monk

'The most important thing that education can develop is compassion towards our fellow beings. I heartily applaud Prof. Achyuta Samanta for choosing to offer his humanitarian service.'

—Sri Mata Amritanandamayi Devi (Amma)
Spiritual Leader, Humanitarian and Chancellor of
Amrita Vishwa Vidyapeetham

'KISS is located in the ancient region of Kalinga, which taught the world the value of *yog* (meditation), not *yudh* (war), and Prof. Samanta embodies this spirit. The virtues of Lord Jagannath guide KISS's transformative journey—from *Jagannath* to *Jaganhaath*.

I believe in the spirit of India and our faith in a divine plan—KISS is a manifestation of this plan. It is not just an educational campus but an epitome of compassion, flowing as a *Daya Nadi* (river of compassion) and *Seva Nadi* (river of service). Prof. Samanta is a true role model, focused on selflessness and giving (*baantna*) rather than accumulation (*batorna*).'

—His Holiness Pujya Swami Chidanand Saraswati Maharaj
Spiritual Leader and President of
Parmarth Niketan Ashram

'At KISS, I feel that the Universe wants me here. This place is a wonder. Dr Samanta, you are an ideal for politicians, social workers and religious leaders. KISS is Karmabhoomi.'

—Swami Suryaprabha
Minister of Religion, Brahmarishi Mission,
United Kingdom

'Dr Samanta is a great humanitarian who truly cares for people and deserves to give humanitarian awards. I want to express my gratitude for receiving the 10th KISS Humanitarian Award from him. To me, this is no less than the Nobel Prize.'

—His Holiness the Dalai Lama
Spiritual Leader of Tibet and Nobel Peace Laureate

'Dr Samanta is approaching a stature that transcends the definitions of a social worker, educationalist or philanthropist. Through his selfless and boundless efforts, he has risen to a spiritual high, defined by his deep compassion for people.'

—Ramesh Oza
Spiritual Leader, Educationalist and Humanitarian

'Dr Samanta is doing work that is close to God—educating children and feeding people.'

—Pujya Ishwarcharan Swami
International Convenor, BAPS Swaminarayan Sanstha

Acknowledgements

The concept of the Art of Giving came to my mind in 2013. Since then, we have institutionalized it. I have long wanted to write a book on its philosophy, the actions it inspires, and its key components. The Art of Giving is nothing new; I am not an avid reader, so everything in this book comes from my personal experiences—of struggle and deprivation, of those whose kindness sustained my family, and of how I, in turn, have strived to give and spread happiness. It has taken me a decade to pen this book, which now serves as both a dossier and a ready reckoner for the Art of Giving.

I would like to express my gratitude to Dr Satyendra Patnaik for his insights into the religious aspects of giving and for making me aware of many tenets of kindness and compassion. He also helped formalize the concept into its early framework. Under his guidance, the Art of Giving has been taught as a course in several universities across India and Taiwan.

I would also like to acknowledge the late Shrikant Rath, who initially transcribed my dictations and created a video on the Art of Giving, narrated in his wonderful voice. I have preserved it as a tribute to his memory.

I am equally grateful to noted journalist Dr D.N. Singh, who has repeatedly shared valuable insights on the contemporary aspects of giving.

My thanks also go to UNESCO MGIEP (United Nations Educational, Scientific and Cultural Organization – Mahatma Gandhi Institute for Peace and Sustainable Development) and their Compassionate Integrity Training. This programme helped me explore many aspects of the Art of Giving in a structured and profound way—including Compassion, Gratitude, Kindness, Empathy and Discernment.

My sister Iti has been an invaluable support. She vividly remembers many instances I had forgotten and possesses the rare gift of putting them into words with clarity. This book would not have been possible without her.

I am also grateful to Rupa Publications for encouraging me to write my second book—this time on the Art of Giving—following my first book *My Hero, My Mother.*

Last but not least, I thank all the fans and followers of the Art of Giving who have, for years, urged me to write this book.